Teamworking

Ann Rippin

T0341559

- ■ Fast track route to getting the most from teams and teamworking

- ■ Covers the key areas of teamworking, from developing an existing team and building highly effective new teams to virtual teaming and teams in the global economy

- ■ Examples and lessons from some of the world's most successful businesses, including Southwest Airlines, the Mayo Clinic and Hitachi, and ideas from the smartest thinkers, including Warren Bennis, Meredith Belbin, Ken Blanchard and Jon R. Katzenbach

- ■ Includes a glossary of key concepts and a comprehensive resources guide

PEOPLE

09.05

essential management thinking at your fingertips

First published 2002 by
Capstone Publishing (a Wiley company)
8 Newtec Place
Magdalen Road
Oxford OX4 1RE
United Kingdom
http://www.capstoneideas.com

CIP catalogue records for this book are available from the British Library and the US Library of Congress

ISBN 978-1-84112-234-2

This book is printed on acid-free paper

Substantial discounts on bulk quantities of Capstone books are available to corporations, professional associations and other organizations. Please contact Capstone for more details on +44 (0)1865 798 623 or (fax) +44 (0)1865 240 941 or (e-mail) info@wiley-capstone.co.uk

Contents

Introduction to ExpressExec

ExpressExec is 3 million words of the latest management thinking compiled into 10 modules. Each module contains 10 individual titles forming a comprehensive resource of current business practice written by leading practitioners in their field. From brand management to balanced scorecard, ExpressExec enables you to grasp the key concepts behind each subject and implement the theory immediately. Each of the 100 titles is available in print and electronic formats.

Through the ExpressExec.com Website you will discover that you can access the complete resource in a number of ways:

» printed books or e-books;
» e-content – PDF or XML (for licensed syndication) adding value to an intranet or Internet site;
» a corporate e-learning/knowledge management solution providing a cost-effective platform for developing skills and sharing knowledge within an organization;
» bespoke delivery – tailored solutions to solve your need.

Why not visit www.expressexec.com and register for free key management briefings, a monthly newsletter and interactive skills checklists. Share your ideas about ExpressExec and your thoughts about business today.

Please contact elound@wiley-capstone.co.uk for more information.

Introduction

Why teams are important and why they will be even more important in the new global and electronic economy.

For more years now than most of us care to remember we have been told that people are an organization's greatest asset. This has been a standard line in many annual company reports which gave the names of all the chief officers of the organization but lumped all those lower down the hierarchy together as an anonymous mass. Mention this to human resource management professionals, though, and you will either get a wise nod of recognition or a strained grin of resignation. We say we value people, but we then do little to translate this value into practice. The same is true of teamworking. We know that people working together can move mountains, but we are not quite sure how to manage the process and so we continue to put people into workgroups and hope that by some strange alchemy a team will appear.

There are many factors in today's environment which mean that this will have to change. If we take an overview of what is happening at a macro level we can see that unlocking the power of a good team is likely to provide one of the most sustainable forms of competitive advantage available to organizations today.

LEANER, FITTER ORGANIZATIONS

Hardly any manager today faced with a problem can consider recruiting an extra person to solve it. Downsized, right-sized, re-engineered companies find that people as resources are in short supply and yet the volume of work is not diminishing. Fewer people are needed to do the same or more work. Productivity gains are vital and productivity will only come through people working together to produce results. As Jack Welch, chairman of General Electric, put it:

> "We know where productivity, real and limitless, comes from. It comes from challenged, empowered, excited, rewarded teams of people."

It is not just the volume of work that is increasing; the kind of work that people are expected to do is also changing. Highly competitive organizations need to be responsive to their customers and their markets. They need to be fast and flexible, which means constantly reconfiguring workgroups. People need to be able to work together, but they also need to be able to do so quickly. People who can form and work in teams quickly and effectively are likely to be in great demand in the future as more and more work is carried out in project teams and task forces.

One of the consequences of downsizing organizations has been a kind of fragmented quality in what remains. People are a bit lost as the colleagues and departments they used to work with have disappeared. The clever use of teams can help to avoid this feeling of disorientation and disintegration by reintegrating people into a new whole.

MERGERS, ACQUISITIONS, AND JOINT VENTURES

In a globalized world one of the most significant forms of strategic activity is the formation of inter-organizational working. This could be a full-blown merger or acquisition or a specific, targeted joint venture; the point is that organizations can no longer sustain impermeable boundaries. Much of this activity is based on capitalizing on another organization's expertise or resources or access, but making it work comes down to teamwork. Many ventures of this sort fail because people cannot find a way of working together. The joint objectives of the initiative are lost in turf battles, or one company becomes "hollowed out" by the other. It is only through clear objectives and joint working to achieve them that inter-organizational activity has any chance of succeeding.

GLOBALIZATION

As organizations become geographically diverse two things happen. People need to work with others who are working in different locations and time zones, and they need to be aware of different cultures. This poses special kinds of difficulties for the teamworking that is needed to make the globalized company function.

Technology

Developments in information technology have made it possible for people to work together in a completely different way. Rather than sharing a work space, and possibly similar contracts of employment, virtual teams are becoming more and more common. The attraction of such working arrangements is obvious: expertise can be drawn from all sources as and when it is needed at greatly reduced fixed costs, but the problems come in managing these remote teams.

Increased competition

Theoretically all organizations have access to similar technology and are bound by the same legislative framework, which means that in one sense they compete on a level playing field. A solution to potential stagnation and decline is the learning organization. This concept suggests that organizations need to be able to scan and learn from their environment. They need to be able to store, retrieve, and share the tacit and explicit knowledge of their employees. For this kind of information flow to work there has to be a team effort. Knowledge management simply cannot work unless it is based on teamwork from inputting the information to building the systems' infrastructure. An organization which does not have a team culture simply will not have high enough levels of trust to make knowledge management and organizational learning work.

Similarly, innovation and creativity are often proposed as a way of ensuring competitive advantage. While teamwork cannot necessarily produce creativity, group problem-solving and creativity techniques have repeatedly resulted in new ideas and process improvements. Synergy comes from teamwork. In addition, if the solitary star worker does come up with a creative idea it requires a team to take that idea and turn it into an innovation. The implementation of creativity is almost never an individual act.

Systems thinking

Peter Senge popularized the idea of systems thinking in *The Fifth Discipline*, but writers on total quality management had long realized that individuals can never outperform the system they are in. Individual star performers are vital for many organizations, but they need active support from a team behind the scenes. This invisible work has long been undervalued, but it is the glue which makes systems work and ensures that work itself gets done.

People at work

All the factors listed above suggest that the context for work is changing fast; the problem is that people are not changing with it. Technologically we might be in the twenty-first century but emotionally and psychologically, the evidence suggests, we are still in the Stone Age. It is fashionable to discredit Maslow's hierarchy of needs which suggests that we move from needing food and shelter, through the need for socialization up to moments of self-actualization, but it appears to be the case that people genuinely like and need to work with other people. There seems to be an in-born desire for affiliation, which is why solitary confinement or shunning people is such a terrible punishment. People like the social side of work. Those who don't are often seen as odd by their colleagues. Many freelancers who return to organizations say that they did so because they needed colleagues. This social function of work may become even more important as people experience the fragmentation of their lives that comes with the breakdown of traditional communities and family units. It is also the case that people in large organizations often like to experience the sense of belonging that comes from small workgroups. Again, it is clear that people want to work together, but translating that impulse into highly efficient workgroups is not easy.

Implications for managers

All of the above factors are increasing the need for teamworking at a macro level, but what are the implications for individual managers in organizations? Essentially, the effective use of teams will make the individual manager's life easier through the benefits it delivers. These include:

» Greater productivity
» Increased motivation
» More likelihood of synergy and creativity
» Reduced turnover
» Improved communication
» Better use of resources
» Higher quality decision making
» Better working atmosphere.

And, just possibly, as anyone who has worked in a great team will know, there is also the experience of working in an environment where there is a buzz in the air and work becomes a pleasure rather than a burden! As the founders of Ben and Jerry's Ice Cream put it:

> "No one at Ben and Jerry's should feel alone or apart. When one of us needs help, we reach out to help. People from outside feel our energy when they visit us. We have a zest for life, a sense of humor, and we enjoy one another's company. We share the excitement of succeeding at the game of business and we'll try to have fun while we do it."

Liberal amounts of teamworking can help to build and maintain this kind of atmosphere.

What is Teamworking?

» What is a team and how is it different from a workgroup?
» What sorts of teams are there?

The idea of teamworking is very simple, so simple, in fact, that most people take their understanding of it for granted. This is dangerous as it leads people to think that they understand and "do" teamworking when what they are really doing is group working. Almost everyone has had the experience of being in a meeting with a group of other people and being expected to produce something, or of being faced with a new group of colleagues and expected to work collaboratively. This is not teamwork but *ad hoc* group work.

Probably the best definition of the difference is given by Jon R. Katzenbach and Douglas K. Smith. They begin by exploring the confusion over the definition of the word "team:"

> "Why define 'team'? The primary reason is to clarify what we mean by team because the word conveys different things to different people. Some think entirely of sports, where coaching, 'individual bests,' and practicing hard to win matter most. Some think about teamwork values like sharing and cooperating, and helping one another. Some think that any group that works together is a team; and some think primarily of two-person pairings like those found in marriage and partnership."

They clearly differentiate between a real team and what they call "a mere group of people with a common assignment" in the following way:

> "A team is a small number of people with complementary skills who are committed to a common purpose, performance goals, and an approach for which they hold themselves mutually accountable."

Katzenbach and Smith insist that teams are interdependent: that is, the job could not be done if one member of the team were permanently missing. There is an element of mutuality. Workgroups, by contrast, are groups of individuals who work together and have a single leader. They are more individualized, like a professional practice of lawyers. Katzenbach and Smith define single-leader workgroups in the following way:

''This is a group for which there is no significant incremental performance need or opportunity that would require it to become a team. The members interact primarily to share information, best practices, or perspectives and to make decisions to help each individual perform within his or her area of responsibility. Beyond that there is no realistic or truly desired 'small group' common purpose, incremental performance goals, or joint work-products that call for either a team approach or mutual accountability.''

According to Katzenbach and Smith, there are six team basics:

» Small number of people (less than 12)
» Complementary skills
» Common purpose
» Common set of specific purpose goals
» Commonly agreed upon working approach
» Mutual accountability.

Patricia J. Addesso also has a checklist of what makes a team. A team, she argues:

» Sets goals.
» Analyzes and solves problems.
» Implements the solutions.
» Feels responsible for its output.

It is important, she insists, to define a team in terms of its outcomes, what it *does* rather than what it is. This is a theme of almost all the writers on teams and teamwork. Some people try to define team spirit, which is a highly elusive concept. You know when you are in a team with a high level of team spirit, but it is very difficult to explain what it is and how it might be generated. It is easier to concentrate on what we can say about teams, and the three key issues appear to be:

» There are two or more individuals involved.
» Those individuals share a clear understanding of what they are trying to achieve and why.
» They understand that they stand no chance of achieving it if they do not work together.

These are the basic requirements of teamworking, but sometimes teams transcend this adequate level of performance and become high-performance teams. Katzenbach and Smith comment:

> "This is a group that meets all the conditions of real teams and has members who are also deeply committed to one another's personal growth and success. That commitment usually transcends the team. The high-performance team significantly outperforms all other like teams, and outperforms all reasonable expectations given its membership."

They concede that there are not that many examples of high-performance teams but that they are "a powerful possibility and an excellent model for all real and potential teams."

Addesso states that high-performance teams have characteristics that set them apart from ordinary teams:

» High levels of communication
» Trust
» Optimism
» High expectations of themselves
» Participation by all members
» Dedication to common goals.

Most of these are affective or psychological processes rather than work structures and procedures.

This dissection of what a team is might seem like using a sledge-hammer to crack a walnut. We all know what a team is, we have all been in them, and know how they feel. Why is it so important to define them? The answer is that although we know about teams from our own life experiences we are often unable to get them to work in our organizations. They are such natural units of operation that we take them for granted and expect disparate groups of people to be able to make them work. Harvey Robbins and Michael Finley's book, *Why Teams Don't Work*, attempts to strip away the mystique of teamworking and present the simplest possible definition:

"A team is easily defined. It is people doing something together. It could be a hockey team making a power play; a research team unraveling an intellectual riddle; a rescue team pulling a child from a burning building; or a family making a life for itself.

"The something part that a team does isn't what makes it a team; the together part is."

Some of the writers we have already mentioned would probably dispute this, arguing that the together part is warm and fuzzy and that concentrating on the purposeful something part is more likely to bring results. But again, anyone who has worked in a really effective team will know that that feeling of being in something together is vital.

TYPES OF TEAMS

Modern organizations have a whole vocabulary in place about teams and teamworking. We talk about project teams, task forces, buzz groups, self-managed teams, steering groups, cross-functional teams, quality circles, virtual teams, customer service support teams, management teams, special committees, standing committees, skunk works, spark groups, and tiger teams. The list is seemingly endless. The most useful framework, though, is probably Katzenbach and Smith's admirably simple trio of terms: teams that make or do things, teams that recommend things, and teams that manage things. In order to get the most out of teams it is important to use this simple framework to establish whether or not you really need a team, and, if so, what you want it to do. Absolute clarity about the function of the team, which cannot be separated from the work you expect it to do, is essential if the team is to have clear and sensible objectives. And without these you cannot monitor team performance and then you have no way of gauging team effectiveness.

Teams that do or make things

The vast majority of teams are set up to produce something – goods or services. This should come as a relief to almost everyone. While it is great for managers to have groups of dynamic, innovative problem solvers, most of the time we need to get the job done. These teams often have a long lifespan, which means that they might have a number of different members during their existence. Once more, however, it is worth repeating that we need to be very clear about what that job is and what standards need to be attained. Vagueness about objectives might sound empowering for some managers but it can end up confusing people. One group that I worked with in a troubled multinational had had the brief "Do Korea." As their team leader said, "How will we know when we've done it, let alone if we've done it well?"

Teams that recommend things

Many special project teams fall into this category. They are set up to research certain areas or to improve processes or to come up with some innovative solutions. Once more there needs to be a very clear remit when these kind of teams are set up. Are they short-term project groups or are they long-term think tanks? People in them need to know, especially if they are successful and start to attract a certain glamor and prestige. At this point the members might seek to prolong their lifespan long beyond any useful purpose they might serve. They might also be resistant to taking on new members who will give them the fresh ideas they need to be effective. It is also vital to be honest with people. The group set up to research a move to new premises might become a little disenchanted if they discover that the preferred option all along is a business park 20 minutes away from the operation manager's home. It is also not advisable to put off making difficult decisions by setting up a subcommittee. Being asked to join the advisory group on car parking is career suicide. This points to the useful lesson that the biggest challenge for this kind of team is often the handover to the implementation team which comes into the making or doing category.

Teams that manage things

These teams are specifically set up to run things, and need to be politically adept. Managing outsourced services is a case in point. Outsourcing often offends people who formerly had control over some area of the organization's business and some of the aggrieved may seek to sabotage this team's best efforts. Senior management teams also come under this heading. The problem here is that those right at the top of organizations are very often a team in name only. Most of them have reached senior positions by being competent at their jobs as individuals. Solo stars often have a temperamental inability to cooperate and collaborate in a way that is vital for an interdependent team. Rugged individuals do not usually make good team players. This is not necessarily a problem unless the group decide to pursue teamworking as an ideal. People lower down the hierarchy (however flat) will spot the "don't do as I do, do as I say" wobble and will act accordingly. With teamworking, as with everything else, senior managers need to walk the talk.

Evolution of Teamworking

» Traces the development of teams from the earliest days of organizations up to the present.
» Examines experience in the United States, Britain, Europe, and Asia.

The history of teamworking is as old as social organization itself. The family, either nuclear or extended, is a team structure in that its members are interdependent, meet together fairly regularly, and have a clear sense of purpose – their mutual well-being. This ideal is not always seen in reality, and the existence of family therapy and other counseling facilities indicates that sometimes the family is a dysfunctional team. Nevertheless, the ideal remains intact.

The team, then, is a familiar structure for getting work done. This is reinforced by our culture. Myths and legends are full of examples of teamworking. The legend of Arthur and the Knights of the Round Table is an example with a dire warning about what happens if your team loses sight of its original objective and gives the competition (Mordred) the opportunity to take over. The story of Robin Hood and his Merry Men gives us a blueprint of how to run a successful team. The objective is clear: protect the territory from the evil Prince John and his lackey, the Sheriff of Nottingham, until the rightful king, Richard the Lionheart, returns from the crusades. The team is interdependent: Robin Hood provides the brains and the prowess with bow and arrow, Little John provides the brawn, Allan-a-Dale provides the entertainment, and Friar Tuck keeps an eye on the processes and procedures. Once the rightful king returns and the job is done the team disbands.

While myths and legends express certain nuggets of truth about human experience, historical events are also instructive. The Roman Empire, arguably one of the greatest organizations that has ever existed, was made possible and sustained by the Roman legions. The key to the legions' success was discipline, both in terms of how they trained and how they used field intelligence. In battle the ordinary Roman soldier was utterly dependent on the two men standing on either side, which meant that the smooth functioning of the whole was far more important than individual heroic prowess. Individual skills were vital, but these were functional. There was a very clear set of objectives – to defeat the enemy for the greater glory of Rome – and this was fully comprehended and shared by everyone. The whole enterprise was carried out in the context of a culture that supported it, which was one of militarism, imperialism, and hierarchical distribution of power. This in turn led to an understanding of the value of logistics in an age of limited communications technology which would impress many modern operations managers. But what swung the balance in the Romans' favor and allowed them to capitalize on their core competencies to gain and sustain competitive advantage was their ability to learn from their enemies' superior technology and to integrate it into their own battle plans and strategies. There are many explanations of why the Empire eventually crumbled, but the one currently holding sway is that it was lack of a unified vision and infighting among the politicians back in Rome which caused the infrastructure to disintegrate. The military metaphor is still powerful in business, particularly its emphasis on the glamor of victory, but the Roman example is instructive for suggesting that more mundane things lead to success than individual heroics.

TEAMWORKING IN ORGANIZATIONS

Early years

Teams are basic units of organization. Teamworking was an essential component of the domestic economy before industrialization. Families would work together either on the land or in cottage industries. Things began to change with the Industrial Revolution as people began to lead lives less regulated by daylight hours and the seasons than by the demands of machines.

With the rise of machine production came an interest in efficiency. The ideas of Adam Smith in *The Wealth of Nations* (1776) were highly influential. Smith was the first to argue that specialization and subdivision of work, and more particularly individualization of tasks, lead to greater efficiency. Smith argued that minimizing the number of component tasks in a process and the development of specialized workers led to greater dexterity in those individuals which would in turn speed up production. Interestingly, Smith argued that this approach to work design would also lead to greater innovation in the invention of more, improved machines. This fragmentation of work, as it has come to be known, has had a huge impact on how we think about work. Skilled workers doing specific tasks is part of received wisdom about how to build an organization, so that we have separate departments in most organizations to deal with particular areas of the business. While we might think that this has been rejected in recent years, it is still unthinkable for most of us that we might work in an organization where there was no separate accounts, personnel, or IT department.

Two other thinkers were highly influential in early organization theory. In the United States Frederick Taylor became fascinated by the possibility of improving the production lines being used at organizations like the Ford Motor Company. His great work, *The Principles of Scientific Management*, was published in 1911. Taylor was one of the earliest advocates of a highly rational approach to work: that is, work was broken down into individual tasks which were timed as they were performed by the most skilled worker available. Any superfluous movements were eliminated. This then became the standard for that task. All the other tasks were timed and an optimum time for the whole was calculated. This was the beginning of time and motion study. In addition to this, Taylor insisted that there was no such thing as individual skill, and that any worker could be trained to do any task. He was obsessed with eliminating what he called "soldiering" which we might term "malingering" and, while he saw it as the manager's job to find out what motivated individuals and to act accordingly, he also believed that management was about discipline and control. Workers were not supposed to use their initiative. Furthermore, he saw worker fraternization as a waste of time leading to inefficiency. Teamwork did not figure in Taylor's rational, scientific universe.

In Europe, Henri Fayol was arguably the first person to try to define management. In contrast to Taylor he thought that managers were more than just overseers and he insisted on their role in creating and sustaining *esprit de corps*. But like Taylor, Fayol was concerned with the division of an organization's activities (in his case into technical, commercial, financial, security, accounting, and management), and of work into discrete tasks so that the individual worker could concentrate on a limited set of tasks and thus increase productivity through the development of expertise. Fayol's *General and Industrial Management* of 1916 was as influential in Europe as Taylor's work was in the United States. His success is an early example of people clamoring to read corporate success stories as his theories were based on his work of turning round a failing French mining company.

Thus, by the middle of the twentieth century production lines were turning out goods in accordance with the rational principles of atomized work. These principles became embedded assumptions about how work should be organized to the point where they became transparent. What challenged this orthodoxy was the unexpected success of Japanese companies in the United States as US industry went into decline. Interest began to shift to Japanese management methods, in particular total quality management.

Total quality management

One of the notable features of TQM is its use of teams, particularly in the guise of quality circles. Essentially, a quality circle consists of a small group of workers who meet in their own time to work with a supervisor on solving a specific work problem. The group might comprise a work team, but it might also have experts who are external to the team and contribute some particular knowledge or expertise. By the 1980s there had been an explosion of quality circles. The advent of quality circles, or quality improvement teams, as they were sometimes called, marked a significant shift in how teams were viewed and used in organizations. There was a move away from seeing workers as cogs in a machine and managers as engineers keeping that mighty machine going, and toward seeing managers as supporters and facilitators of teams of people who knew the best way to improve both work processes and the organization itself. At least that was the theory. Many quality circles failed because the culture into which they were transplanted was unable to sustain them. To work, quality circles require resources, top management support, a long lead time, well-trained facilitators, and a cultural shift toward workers giving up their unpaid free time to attend. If any one of these elements is missing it is unlikely that the quality circle will work.

The new wave of US management thinkers

Although quality circles fell somewhat into disrepute, they did improve the status of the team as a structure for improving work. Teamworking was back on the list of desirable organizational attributes. By the 1980s and 1990s empowerment had become a new organizational concern, and with it the idea of self-managed teams. These two decades really saw the rise of management gurus, particularly US writers such as Tom Peters and Robert Waterman, Richard Pascale, and Rosabeth Moss

Kanter. They all insisted that ordinary workers had a great deal to contribute to improving their individual jobs and thus organizational performance. They claimed that workers knew more about the work than anyone else, were closer to customers, and were full of ideas about how to bring about useful lasting change. What was needed was for managers to give workers a clear understanding of what their jobs were and how they fitted into the organization's mission, the training to perform them, and then room to operate. Managers had to trust their people and give them power to innovate and bring about change. One of the main contributions of writers like Peters and Kanter was to bring about a shift in thinking that teamwork was important only in manufacturing industries. They insisted that people everywhere in all organizations should work collectively to bring about the levels of customer service that would lead to sustainable profitability and market share.

The European contribution

There were other, less well-known investigations of teamworking. In the 1940s, for example, Eric Trist and K.W. Bamforth (an ex-miner) studied working practices in Durham coal mines in the north of England. They discovered that miners spontaneously organized themselves into what we would probably now call self-managed teams in response to dangerous working conditions. Their managers wanted them to work in a rationalized, "scientific" way in which mining became highly specialized and mechanized. Miners were supposed to work in shifts during which each group would work at one stage of the process only, and each miner was restricted to one part of the task in the fragmented way familiar from Taylor's theories. Under this system the miners would have been unable to develop a range of skills. The miners rejected this and insisted on working in composite rather than specialist teams which were multi-skilled and self-selecting. They undertook the whole coal-getting cycle on each shift. And, in a way that foreshadows today's empowered, self-managing teams, they had no leader or supervisor, but elected representatives to liaise on their behalf with their management. They were paid on a common paynote which assumed that all members made equal contributions rather than through a piecework system. They grouped themselves into units of about 40 people, and scheduled and allocated work for themselves, which allowed them to develop a range of skills. Trist and Bamforth called this "composite autonomous group working," and wrote about it in glowing terms.

Teamworking is also associated with cellular manufacturing, which involves putting together all the people, materials, and equipment necessary to make a range of broadly similar products. This approach to factory layout was introduced in the early 1950s and continues in many factories today. Teamwork obviously supports the rationale behind it, namely that of working together to increase productivity based on product autonomy. This method of working has much in common with Japanese-style manufacturing methods. But it also points to one of the key lessons about teamworking: just putting people together in a group and expecting them to become a team is unlikely to be successful. Good teamwork requires planning.

Several other initiatives have promoted teamworking. The Netherlands and Scandinavia in the second half of the twentieth century both adopted autonomous workgroup practices. The Volvo plants at Kalmar and Uddevalla are well-known examples of the use of teams to reduce the routine nature of work by empowering the work force and paying careful attention to ergonomic considerations in plant layout. The repetitive nature of much manufacturing work and the attendant boredom and stress led to the Quality of Working Life movement in Britain and the United States in the 1970s. Autonomous group working was seen as one of the best ways to give some control back to the work force and to make work more satisfying as people worked on the whole process rather than fragmented parts. In Germany in the early 1970s the Humanization of Work initiative involved companies in a wide variety of industries experimenting with worker empowerment including autonomous workgroups. Volkswagen is one of the best-known participants in this experimental approach.

Many of these experiments were just that – experiments. The Volvo plant in Uddevalla, for example, was closed. The experiments were undertaken as concepts of lean manufacturing and business process re-engineering began to gain ground. Teamworking is not a short-term answer to productivity and profitability problems. It has a long lead time as the team forms and grows. It is not the best tool for a short-term return on investment. But once the downsizing has taken place and further cuts would be suicidal, teamworking is probably the only answer as experience suggests that creativity and innovation can only be operationalized through groups of people working together with a common purpose. Even if this were not the case, there is still a moral imperative for teamworking and the job enrichment its working processes appear to bring.

The European and US initiatives described above stemmed from a desire to increase democracy at work and to make routine work more bearable. Both the need to compete through innovation and the increasing demands of people in the work force to be treated like human beings rather than cogs in a machine mean that teamwork is likely to be of vital importance in the twenty-first century.

IMPORTANT DATES IN THE HISTORY OF TEAMWORKING

- » 1776: Smith's *The Wealth of Nations*
- » 1911: Taylor's *The Principles of Scientific Management*
- » 1916: Fayol's *General and Industrial Management*
- » 1940s: Trist and Bamforth's work on Durham miners and composite autonomous group working
- » 1950s: Cellular manufacturing
- » 1962: Kaoru Ishikawa's quality circles
- » 1970s: Humanization of Work and Quality of Working Life initiatives
- » 1982: Peters and Waterman's *In Search of Excellence*
- » 1983: Kanter's *The Change Masters*

The E-Dimension

» Examines the importance of virtual teams in modern organizations and gives hints and pointers on how to make them work.
» Considers the vital role that teams will play in knowledge management and how teams are likely to become a key resource for competitive advantage in the future.

There are two main ways in which the Internet and ICT (information communications technology) in general will impact on teams and teamworking. The first, and most obvious, one is the development of virtual teams. The second is the vital connection between teams and knowledge management.

VIRTUAL TEAMS

Virtual teams are an inevitable part of the new economy with its emphasis on speed, responsiveness, adding value, and flexibility. The trend to minimize the core of organizations and to locate as much processing as possible outside in the periphery also leads to the increased use of virtual teams. Portfolio workers, people who do not have one job but work on a variety of projects simultaneously, almost certainly work in one or more virtual teams.

Virtual teams are characterized as follows:

» Groups of people who work together on a project but are remote from the organization.
» They are often in geographically diverse locations with all the implications that brings in cultural and time dislocations.
» They may or may not meet periodically in one location for face-to-face discussions.
» They communicate electronically and share resources which are generally available on-line.
» They are probably, although not necessarily, a short-term team brought together to work on a specific time-bounded project, although they can also be a new form of outworkers sitting in their electronic cottages working long term for one employer.
» They often have highly specialized and expert members whose time is at a premium.
» Team members are probably working on a number of different projects and project teams simultaneously.
» They may or may not have a team leader situated in the core organization.

Ironically, while they do not fit the received idea of a team as a group of people who work together in close physical proximity getting to know each other's foibles and strengths, virtual teams can be truer teams than conventional ones. They are generally interdependent. Members are chosen for their blend of skills and therefore the team could not do its work if one member were missing. They are frequently highly focused on the end result, particularly if they are time-bounded working on one particular project with a deadline. They have clear performance measures. The blend of clearly identified deliverables and the feedback on performance made possible by ICT mean that it is sometimes easier to measure performance for a virtual team which is in some ways isolated from its "host" organization than it is to monitor a conventional team.

Examples of virtual teams are:

» People working from home inputting data or providing customer services via a computer and a modem. They may or may not deal directly with customers.
» A research team with members in different laboratories or university departments throughout the world.
» A salesforce working for one company but within clearly defined geographical limits. They might meet periodically or all contact might be via phone calls and email.
» A professional firm with subdivisions handling specialized areas of business. These can be located anywhere in the world but they would maintain a database of information which would benefit other members of the firm, and would offer support and expertise via ICT.
» A small firm of associates who may never all meet but who will coalesce into small groups to work on one project, then disband, and move on to the next.

Virtual teams offer organizations many benefits, particularly if they find change difficult. Great lumbering monoliths can find it difficult to change direction quickly in order to capture a market or capitalize on a good idea. Virtual teams, through the intelligent use of ICT, can make rapid change possible within even the most moribund organization, as long as such organizations have the will and the capacity to make teams work – something which is far from certain.

Virtual teams allow organizations to make rapid responses because they offer a way to bring together custom-made teams without necessarily having all the necessary expertise in-house. The teams can be made up of people already inside the organization but they can also include freelancers from outside. These freelancers are likely to be contract staff such as IT professionals, or consultants, or other experts. They might also include people who have left the organization but continue to have some connection to it, such as people who have taken early retirement but are retained on a consultancy basis. The virtual, contingent team allows organizations to draw on a wide pool of talent without having to keep it on the payroll. People might be paid on a fee per job basis or on a retainer. This is likely to be a cost-effective option as it can avoid on-costs such as pensions and insurance of various kinds, and it will probably also mean that savings can be made on accommodation costs. But cost should be a secondary consideration to speed of response and the ability to target customer needs precisely.

Virtual teams also offer flexibility – they can be created and disbanded quickly as needs or business opportunities arise. They can provide geographical representation or market intelligence without the need for a physical presence in a particular company. This is similar to the agent system used by large organizations during colonial rule. It gives access to expert knowledge of local conditions and avoids potentially expensive or embarrassing mistakes caused by lack of sensitivity to local culture and custom. At the very least a network of potential team members can offer sophisticated, targeted intelligence gathering both at home and abroad. It can also develop internal networks as people in the organization work with each other in virtual teams, and this in turn provides the ideal platform for knowledge management.

The opportunity to join virtual teams can also benefit individuals. The freelance team member can pick and choose assignments and can use the opportunity to be a virtual member of a prestigious organization as a way of strengthening both their portfolio of work and their list of clients. It also helps to break down the sense of isolation that many freelancers report. It is unlikely that many people would make a career out of being a virtual team member, but the increase of such working arrangements means that virtual teamworking is already making a substantial contribution to the mix of jobs of many portfolio workers.

As with many working practices, however, these advantages to organizations can quickly become means of exploiting their work force if care is not taken. A flexible work force can be a disposable work force, and organizations need to think carefully before shattering the relationship of trust which is necessary to make any team work.

There are also operational issues which can adversely affect the virtual team's performance. The fact that the operation is at arm's length can mean that there is a lack of clarity around the project, and the isolation from other team members can lead to a loss of common purpose. Unless the ground rules are established very clearly at the outset there can be confusion about roles in the team. In one virtual team that I worked on I understood that I was engaged to evaluate a particular program, whereas the team leader expected me to contribute to its design. I considered this to be a clash of interests for the client, and this led to some difficult conference calls as we sorted out the confusion. The problem could have been avoided with sufficient ground work on roles and responsibilities at the outset. There can also be conflicting local and global priorities in virtual teams. Is the loyalty to the immediate local concern or to the geographically remote parent organization? There are also the inevitable communication difficulties, particularly if members of the team have varying levels of proficiency in whichever language is chosen, and there are possibly legal differences to be overcome.

There are a number of lessons to be learned from this:

» Be very clear about the project's goals. What do you expect to be the outcome and when? Make sure that these are understood by everyone by setting them out clearly and finding some compelling way of reinforcing them without boring people. Publishing deadlines, agreed action plans, and responsibilities is likely to reduce the margin for error. Also consider publishing progress sheets or news sheets showing what has been achieved, future forecasts, or problems dealt with.

» Be very clear about roles and responsibilities. Empowerment and job enrichment are all very well in a long-term project but how much of them can you afford to have in a geographically diverse team operating in a number of cultures which might be very different to your own? Or in a team which is contracted to provide a certain level of service to a customer with a very clear and tight specification?

» Be very clear about where decisions will be made. Will they be delegated to those out in the field or will they be the responsibility of those at the center? How will they be made? Does everyone know this and understand the difference between participative and consultative decision making?

» Think very carefully about project management, both in its pure sense and in the day-to-day management of the project. Virtual teams' greatest problem is duplication of effort. Consider how you will set up your archiving or knowledge management system to avoid this.

» Invest in face-to-face meeting. Commentators on virtual teams agree that some contact is vital for the team to work well together. It is very difficult to distinguish voices on a conference call unless you have met. Video conferencing is a substitute, but face-to-face occasionally is best.

Managing virtual teams is a particular skill. It requires the skills of standard team leadership, but with an additional focus on even sharper clarity of expectation and on motivating potentially isolated people.

KNOWLEDGE MANAGEMENT

Knowledge management is now generally acknowledged as a core competency or a critical competitive factor. Organizations spend vast amounts of money on the hard- and software associated with knowledge management, but the key to making it work is the quality of input which in turn depends on people. Knowledge management is an abstraction of the knowledge, tacit and explicit, of the teams which make up an organization. This is a vast subject and it is only possible here to highlight the impact of teamworking on successful management. The main considerations are cultural.

In the case below Jasper Jarlback, the managing partner of the business consulting practice at Arthur Andersen Denmark, defines knowledge management as $(K + P + I)^S$, where K = knowledge, and P = people's ability to exchange information (I) which is exponentially enhanced by the power of sharing (S). The tricky part comes in the sharing because knowledge management can be seen as threatening to many staff. People feel threatened by potential knowledge overload. Knowledge management represents yet more "stuff to read" and so they are disinclined to add to it. They are also reluctant to add to the system and thus to add to the time burdens of their peers. Knowledge management can represent a diminution of the expertise that makes people feel indispensable. Despite the new career in the new economy most people would prefer to avoid redundancy if possible and many feel that sharing their expertise will diminish their job security. Similarly, in the past people have been promoted for personal expertise and this personal competitive advantage is unlikely to be sustainable where knowledge is freely shared. This also highlights the importance of team culture to making the system work. Organizations which reward individual excellence and foster individual profit centers are unlikely to be able to make a collective system like knowledge management work. Finally, ICT can be seen as closet surveillance and people resent being watched. Some knowledge management systems have in-built performance monitoring capabilities which may be resented.

All the above concerns suggest a number of ideas for good practice in knowledge management which hinge on teamwork:

» Recruit for sharing attributes. Rather than trying to change the culture of individualism in existing employees it is worth considering selecting for a sharing orientation.
» Pay close attention to developing a relationship of trust with your team and all employees. People who don't trust won't contribute effectively to knowledge management systems. Do not be tempted to use the system for monitoring purposes unless you tell people that this is what you intend to do.
» Audit what you use the system for. What is key and useful? Allow teams to have some input into the design of the systems they will be asked to use.
» Examine your information processes. People might be right: you might be duplicating documents on your system. Be rigorous in your information audit.
» Demonstrate how a good knowledge management system will make teams' lives easier by improving access to materials to help them do their jobs and serve their customers better.

» Consider push and pull when designing your system. People should use it because they want to use it (pull) rather than because you want them to (push). How can you make it functional and attractive to use?

» Consider the next step in a knowledge-driven learning organization – the community. Try to envisage your organization as a community which looks to the good of the whole while trying to achieve its objectives. Teams are the building blocks of communities.

Information communities are likely to be the future configuration of organizations. David Coleman, managing director of Collaborative Strategies San Francisco, describes them as the apex of the knowledge management pyramid:

"... communities, consciously created and maintained. To us this seems a natural extension of collaboration and managing knowledge, yet we see very few organizations actually taking this step. In terms of intellectual capital, we see these communities as a way not only to preserve this resource, but actually to have access to both the tacit and explicit knowledge in an organization."

Communities need to be nurtured in the same way as teams and if they are going to be a prerequisite of survival in the new economy then team-building expertise is likely to be a key skill.

ARTHUR ANDERSEN DENMARK

Arthur Andersen Worldwide SC is a major international professional services organization. It operates in over 360 locations in 76 countries and has over 82,000 employees. The organization comprises member firms which operate autonomously under the Arthur Andersen umbrella. The capacity for reinventing the wheel is enormous and this made Arthur Andersen a good site for a team-based knowledge management initiative. Indeed, the firm prides itself on having recognized this need and implemented a solution before knowledge management as a concept existed.

Arthur Andersen Denmark was committed to developing a workable system, and while it had to work initially with fairly rudimentary technology, it paid very close attention to the human side of making it work. At the heart of this was an open office concept which was designed to develop teamworking and the sharing which is vital to making knowledge management work. One of the first things to go was the iconic building which housed the firm. While this building had proclaimed solidarity and probity in the early years of the firm a new building which projected a modern image was needed to encourage the desired teamworking atmosphere. In the new building there were to be no individual offices and hot desking and hot phones were introduced. All desks had the capacity to network PCs which were linked to the central Arthur Andersen platform allowing access to centralized information.

People did not respond too well at first to having their personal space removed and a great deal of time had to be spent communicating with them and reassuring them, but the new office layout also led to a more fundamental shift in work organization. It began to break down hierarchies. Carl Dalsgaard, the partner responsible for external knowledge management services, commented:

"One of the best things about Arthur Andersen is the 'one-firm' concept. Arthur Andersen is able to leverage its international expertise in an unrivaled manner. We are only able to do it because we work through teams – teams of all kinds: across practice, across offices and across countries if necessary. As we move from team to team across projects, we form our own informal networks. These networks are reinforced periodically at annual firm-wide or regional meetings and at training courses. You just cannot survive within Arthur Andersen without a good people network!"

What this example demonstrates is that for knowledge management to be successful similar conditions need to apply to those needed for effective teamworking. In particular:

» There needs to be equity of access to the tools to do the job. Teams need tools and in a knowledge management system everyone needs access to the technology to contribute to the system. While there might be an argument for making certain parts of the system available only to certain levels of the hierarchy, everyone needs to feel involved.

» There needs to be a constant emphasis on the importance of teams. This needs to be built into the organizational culture. It cannot be bolted on when teamworking is suddenly important for some major organizational initiative such as knowledge management.

» There needs to be an atmosphere of trust. Teams only work when the members trust each other and the team leader. Knowledge management only works when contributors believe that the information is being used in an open and ethical way. It is hard to persuade people to contribute to a system they think might be used to keep them under surveillance.

The Global Dimension

» Global strategies are likely to come unstuck unless they are supported by good information gathered in global markets. Teams are an effective way to do this.
» Examines how national culture impacts on the likelihood of success in teaming.
» Considers the dilemmas of managing culturally diverse teams in multinational organizations.

Globalization is a familiar concept to most of us. We understand the idea of companies operating throughout the world 24 hours a day. But the truly global, rather than multinational, business is still the exception rather than the rule. Most commentators on globalization see it as a staged process from a company exporting to international markets in the first instance to locating plant and personnel over a wide geographic spread of countries and becoming "internalized." This is what many people, including the Japanese strategy guru, Kenichi Ohmae, call thinking globally and acting locally.

Globalization, in the true sense, means giving autonomy to local subsidiaries to operate independently without much interference from the parent company. A few household names such as Coca-Cola, McDonald's, Microsoft, and Levis can operate without greatly tailoring their products to the local market, but most companies have to produce bespoke versions of their offerings to meet local consumer needs. Some products, such as washing powder, have the potential to go global, but others, such as food, have to respond to local needs. This might seem to be a matter of product development or strategic marketing, but it has implications for teamworking.

Global teamworking takes two forms. It can be virtual teamworking in which teams of people work together to meet their objectives, sharing information and working on it simultaneously, regardless of where they are located geographically, through the use of ICT; or it can be actual teamworking in remote geographical locations. And within the latter category, it can be groups of expatriate workers or integrated groups of expatriates and local people working together in teams. This raises interesting questions about how such teams might be managed.

Figure 5.1 suggests that there is a continuum of opportunities for close management of teams. Close control may or may not be desirable where empowerment and innovation are required, but the continuum highlights some of the main points about global teamworking.

EXPATRIATE TEAMS

These teams take with them the home country and home company's culture intact. There is no need to socialize them and to ensure that they share the same vision as the home company. But, as we shall see, they also run the risk of causing major dissatisfaction in the local

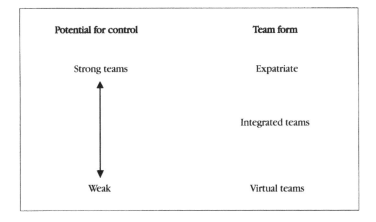

Fig. 5.1

company, and of being stuck with cultural myopia, the inability to see beyond their native mindset. Expatriate teams are most often found in senior management functions.

INTEGRATED TEAMS

Integrated teams may or may not have a team leader from the local country. If they are led by a team leader from the home country, like an expatriate team, they are more likely to take the corporate culture with them.

VIRTUAL TEAMS

As with homeworking, many senior managers are reluctant to trust workers they cannot see, and it is certainly difficult to monitor people working in remote locations in different time zones. Ironically, the very technology which enables virtual working, and therefore a high level of autonomy, can also be used to monitor work to the point of surveillance, in which case the potential for control, and also for a near complete breakdown of trust, is paradoxically greater.

There is far more to globalized teamworking than control, however, and managers need to be aware of the special demands of this way of organizing.

NATIONAL CHARACTERISTICS

One of the components of the Japanese management system which was so closely analyzed in the 1980s and 1990s was teamworking and collegiality. Why was it that it took US car manufacturers a total of 1500 employees to form a product development team whereas it took Japanese car manufacturers only 250 people to produce a more sophisticated design in less time? Western commentators were dismissive of the conformist, unquestioning loyalty to the company, and often baffled when this commitment produced workers who would voluntarily meet outside paid work hours to contribute to quality circles. This was compared unfavorably to the rugged individualism of US and British firms where individual performance counted so highly. The three pillars of Japanese attitudes to their companies – obligation, consensus, and family – obviously contribute to the centrality of teamworking in their organizations. People feel a sense of obligation to their teams. Decision making within them is based on consensus, and members are committed to mutual advantage in a way that Western teams often are not. A standard US/British team model is of a group making it possible for an individual to take center stage. Despite the fact that there are indications that mutuality is breaking down in Japanese society, this kind of individualism would be unthinkable for a Japanese team.

One of the best-known commentators on national characteristics is Geert Hofstede. It is possible to criticize Hofstede for his small sample size from which he generalizes and for the fact that he was only studying one, large, multinational corporation (IBM), but his findings always seem to strike a chord with people. He analyzes national cultures along a number of axes such as strong and weak uncertainty avoidance, masculinity and femininity, and attitudes to authority. With regard to teamworking, Hoftstede's work on individualism versus collectivism is most interesting. He defines it as follows:

"Individualism pertains to societies in which the ties between individuals are loose: everyone is expected to look after himself or herself and his or her immediate family. Collectivism as its opposite pertains to societies in which people from birth onwards are integrated into strong, cohesive ingroups, which throughout people's lifetime continue to protect them in exchange for unquestioning loyalty."

(Hofstede, 1991, p. 51)

This suggests two things:

» Some cultures are more willing to adopt teamworking practices than others.
» Some cultures are more willing than others to adopt self-managed teamwork practices or empowerment than others.

Hofstede ranks the 50 countries in his study according to their orientation towards individualism.

HOFSTEDE'S 12 MOST INDIVIDUALISTIC NATIONAL CULTURES

1 USA
2 Australia
3 Britain
4 Canada
5 The Netherlands
6 New Zealand
7 Italy
8 Belgium
9 Denmark
10 Sweden
11 France
12 Ireland

He also lists the most collectivist cultures.

HOFSTEDE'S 12 MOST COLLECTIVIST NATIONAL CULTURES

1 Guatemala
2 Ecuador
3 Panama
4 Venezuela
5 Colombia
6 Indonesia
7 Pakistan
8 Costa Rica
9 Peru
10 Taiwan
11 South Korea
12 El Salvador

Japan, according to Hofstede's study, is the 22nd most individualistic culture. It would come as no surprise to Hofstede, then, that the Americans and the British have found such difficulties with teamworking, and that Asian companies (Thailand and Singapore were the 13th and 14th most collectivist cultures) should adopt it so willingly. It goes some way toward explaining the British scepticism and resistance to Japanese teamworking principles in Japanese car plants in Britain in the 1980s. In terms of globalization, this work is helpful if it forearms Asian managers trying to instil teamworking principles in resistant British workers, or Western managers faced with perplexed Japanese partners encountering individual performance glory.

ORGANIZATIONAL STRUCTURES

One of the fundamental decisions about how to manage a global organization is how the subsidiaries of the parent company will be structured. There are three basic forms of organization:

» Ethnocentric
» Polycentric
» Geocentric.

Ethnocentrism

The first form to emerge was the ethnocentric. This is where the most important positions are filled by parent company nationals. Thus, at one time, Philips NV had Dutch nationals filling all the senior management positions in its overseas interests. Japanese and South Korean firms such as Toyota, Matsushita, and Samsung have also favored this structure. The form, however, is on the wane because it appears to lead to low morale and productivity leading to high turnover of local staff. The message employees receive is clear: we don't trust you to run our business, and, what's more, no matter how hard you work you will never attain a true position of responsibility and influence. This culture is poisonous to good, effective teamworking, where an atmosphere of trust and respect is vital. In the Philips example, the management team came to be known as the "Dutch Mafia." Ethnocentrism also leads in many cases to the cultural myopia already mentioned. It is the enemy of the diversity necessary for companies to compete in a global economy.

Polycentrism

In this form local nationals hold key positions in the subsidiaries, but the most powerful positions in the home corporate headquarters are still held by home nationals. While this can give the illusion of control, the situation can arise, as Unilever discovered using this organizational form, that local subsidiaries start to go their own way regardless of head office and the ability to manage is actually reduced. The implications for teamworking of this form are less clear, but it is still the case that the nationals in the local jobs would be unlikely to have a great deal of influence on corporate policy, and local cultural norms, pro or anti-teamworking, would be likely to apply.

Geocentrism

In this form the best person is in post regardless of nationality, and the home company has the potential to develop a truly global competent group of managers. This rich diversity is one of the building blocks of great teamworking, and offers the possibility of a global team-based organization.

Light and heavy teams

Within the broader organizational structures just discussed teams can take a variety of forms. One way of thinking about this is to think in terms of "lightweight" and "heavyweight" teams. These terms refer to the weight of management control attached to them. A lightweight team has a self-managing orientation whereas a heavyweight team has much more supervisory input. Obviously some countries where individualism is prominent are likely to want to have a light structure. Workers in other countries, where there is more deference to authority and hierarchy, might be unnerved by too much autonomy. Managers have to be sensitive to these needs. Virtual teams also can be either light and left alone to manage themselves, or heavy in which the enabling technology is used to monitor their work in an obtrusive fashion.

REWARD AND REMUNERATION

Managing globalized companies highlights the challenge of getting reward structures right, but in this case the stakes are particularly high. Finding a way of rewarding teams as opposed to individual performance is difficult but essential if teams in a Western context are to flourish, but the problem is magnified if the team is based overseas. There are a number of difficult questions to face:

» Do we pay our expatriates the same rate as they would get at home? If we don't they might refuse to go, or they might become demotivated. If we do, we risk destabilizing the local economy if we suddenly introduce a whole cadre of what are, to all intents and purposes, millionaires.

» Do we pay the expatriates and the local staff the same rate? If we don't will the locals resent the expats, and will the expats consider the locals naive and exploitable? If we do, what do we do about creating sudden imbalances in wealth?

» Do we compensate for salary discrepancies with some kind of benefits such as cars or accommodation? If so, do we create dependencies and jealousies? Is this another form of cultural imperialism?

These are difficult questions to resolve, and companies have to be creative in setting up incentives for returning expatriate employees.

These can take the form of foreign service premiums which are usually a percentage of basic salary, or various allowances for housing, cost of living, or hardship if the employee is going to an expensive location such as Tokyo. There is also likely to be a benefits package for medical expenses and pensions.

INNOVATION AND DIVERSITY

Throughout this chapter, the idea of the diversity that potentially comes with globalization has been bubbling under the surface. The fact is that many large organizations are increasingly obliged to compete on a global scale. More and more companies have global markets, but not that many companies have managers able to exploit them. This is where teams are vital. If the marketplace is diverse then the team designing the offering needs to reflect that diversity if it is to satisfy customer needs, or, more fundamentally, to avoid huge and costly mistakes.

I worked as a consultant with one large British-based manufacturer and retailer of toiletries and cosmetics which had to scrap a promotional campaign based around Easter but destined for Buddhist countries, with all the expense that waste implies. With a truly global marketing team this would not have happened. There are likely to be some unintended consequences to empowering local teams. If you remove cultural myopia you have to be prepared for teams to come up with business ideas that you had not expected. It is possible, for instance, that a diverse team working on selling batteries to parts of Africa might have come to the same conclusion as inventor Trevor Bayliss – that wind-up or solar-powered radios had a bigger potential market than unsustainable, expensive batteries, and a battery manufacturer might have become a radio manufacturer. Ignoring that idea might leave the door open for the Baylisses of this world to clean up.

BEST PRACTICE

Very few companies would claim to have all the answers about how to develop effective global teams and so conclusions must be drawn from a limited selection of examples, most often in cross-functional product development functions. Even from this small sample, however, it is clear that there are lessons to be learned about making teams work on a global scale.

One of the earliest and best-known examples is the development of the European Ford Escort car in the early 1990s. This was a five-year program led by designers and engineers based in England and Germany. Eventually the team expanded to 1200 people before the car was completed. This might seem too large a group to qualify as a team, but points to the new architecture of the global firm. Small and large exist simultaneously as large organizations work through small teams drawn from all over the world, in this case West European companies and the United States. Ford called this "program management" and it involved new product development started in Europe. The former CEO of Ford, Donald Petersen, comments:

"One of the great advantages of having a team with such diverse talents, both technically and culturally, is that it has the expertise and background to know how customer tastes will vary from France to Belgium, or from Eastern Europe to western Germany."

And Petersen indicates what can be learned from global teamworking as he describes being impressed by the European ability to build teams and facilitate teamworking.

The other model which is frequently seen is to set up a number of research and development units throughout the company to work on either discrete products or technologies. Hewlett Packard has R&D units in Palo Alto, California; Bristol, England; Haifa, Israel; and Tokyo, Japan. Each of these work on new product technologies coordinated by HP's global product division. Microsoft has basic research sites in Redmond, Washington; Cambridge, England; and Silicon Valley, California. These centers work on new technologies such as artificial intelligence which are converted into product improvements or new products by dedicated product groups. Decentralized subsidiaries then work on customizing new products for local markets. This is an essential function for a company selling into the Chinese market, requiring the system to function with Chinese characters and a Chinese interface. Canon, on the other hand, was well known for developing products for the home market which, if successful, were then exported to the rest of the world. This strategy seems less likely to be employed as product lead times are slashed by the use of new technology.

LESSONS LEARNED

» New structures are emerging in the world of global teams as companies pyramid their team structures from local to global.

» Organizations see their ideas and cultures change as they become more global and learn from their subsidiaries rather than trying to control them.

» People close to the customer at a local level have to be allowed input to product design and strategy making. Lip service has been paid to this for years, but in the global economy local teams and the market intelligence they bring cannot be ignored.

» Despite the vast advances in ICT people still need to meet face to face sometimes, and the most senior managers need to "tour the colonies" both for their own benefit and that of their teams.

» Remote teams in particular need a heavyweight champion or sponsor with access to resources and the ability to represent the team to the organizational power brokers if they are to be successful and the organization is to capitalize on their knowledge.

The State of the Art

» Teams as a key strategic resource.
» Teams and mergers, acquisitions and strategic alliances.
» Teams, collaboration, and competition.
» Teams and the new science.
» Team leadership.
» Abuse of teams.
» Great groups and how to create them.

Current work on teams and teamwork, which builds on earlier thinking, is shedding light on what makes teams successful and why they are important by concentrating, broadly, on two areas: sustaining competitive advantage and day-to-day team leadership.

DEVELOPING AND SUSTAINING COMPETITIVE ADVANTAGE THROUGH TEAMWORKING

In the 1990s the resource-based view (RBV) of competitive advantage gained popularity. It stressed that the key to an organization's success is its ability to exploit its heterogeneity, that is the unique bundle of resources and capabilities which allow it to beat its competitors. This contrasts with the previously popular model of the industry-based view which emphasized the importance of choosing an advantageous position in an industry or market from which to compete. The RBV implies that the organization's ability to configure and reconfigure its resources depends on its capabilities – that is, what you've got and how you make it work. Teamworking is a capability which will allow an organization to leverage its resources and good teamworking will allow it to squeeze the maximum return on resources.

One of the major sources of competitive advantage is the ability to innovate and this, as we have seen, is often best achieved through teams. Very few creative people can single-handedly implement their ideas: they need a team to make them work. This is particularly true of technical and scientific endeavors despite the persistent stereotype of the maverick mad scientist inventor. So the ability to work through teams is likely to be an increasingly important prerequisite for reaching strategic objectives.

In order for organizations to capture the benefits of teamworking there needs to be a radical redesign of many organizations. Flatter organizations need to be developed based around workflows to improve customer service, for example, not around functions or tasks. Organizations should be based around teams, not individuals, in order to group together related but previously fragmented tasks. This would give each team access to a larger set of skills, perspectives, and experience. Real teams have complementary skills, common purpose, and mutual accountability and they work toward specific, measurable goals. This implies that teams must be empowered to work toward their goals virtually independently. There needs to be a workable team-based reward structure if collective working is to succeed. Organizations need to be structurally configured to achieve their strategic aims and for many this will mean including teamworking in their strategic thinking.

Also under the heading of strategic imperatives is the increasingly present reality of mergers and acquisitions, joint venture and strategic alliances. Bringing together two or more entities requires everyone in the organization to work with and through people in rapidly changing configurations. Western companies attempting to work with Japanese partners in the 1980s and early 1990s found that they were unable to capitalize on the alliance because they could not work with partners well enough to capture new know-how. They reported being "hollowed out" – their expertise was exploited but they had learned very little in return.

Outsourcing can be a minefield if there is no sense of teamwork and the commitment to a shared aim that it brings. The problems are made worse by the fact that so few senior managers are really able to work together through lack of collaborative experience or a reluctance to share power or a desire to hang on to functional specialisms. But mergers and acquisitions – from the consolidation of multinational consulting houses to merging local schools – seem likely to increase as globalization takes even further hold and the ability to work quickly and effectively in a team with new colleagues becomes a key personal competence.

One of the great business gurus, Peter Drucker, writes in *The Organization of the Future*:

"Increasingly command and control is being replaced by or intermixed with all kinds of relationships, alliances, joint ventures, minority participations, partnerships, know-how, and marketing agreements – all relationships in which no one controls and no one commands. These relationships have to be based on a common understanding of objectives, policies and strategies; on teamwork; and on persuasion – or they do not work at all."

What will give organizations the edge on a playing field made level by IT is the ability to think better with the available data. This requires intelligent people working together on a common problem. This sounds straightforward: we all work for the same organization, we all share the same goals, therefore we will be able to work together for the common aim. This is not necessarily the case. Writers on teamworking are often fascinated by what makes teams fail, and one of the most compelling explanations seems to be the Western world's obsession with rugged individualism.

Toward the end of his life W. Edwards Deming became increasingly interested in the debilitating effects of competition, stating at one of his famous seminars, "America has been sold down the river on competition," and exhorting his listeners to save competition for their competitors and not their internal collaborators.

Robert Reich wrote in the *Harvard Business Review* that entrepreneurship was not, as previously thought, likely to be a product of the single hero, but of the team, and he urged a reframing of the team rather than the individual as a hero. "We need to honor our teams more, our aggressive leaders and maverick geniuses less" he wrote as he stressed the importance of collective entrepreneurship. Reich highlighted a common structure for achievement in organizations, namely that of the "entrepreneurial heroes" and the "industrial drones." The "inspired masters" are glamorous risk-taking figures of daring, imagination, and pluck. They get all the reward and recognition, whereas the "perspired servants" are uninterested and uninteresting, reliable and pliable, but seen as cogs in a large machine that need discipline rather than praise. Reich comments that the entrepreneurial hero and the worker drone together personify the mythic version of how the US economic system works, but, he asserts, this is an obsolete myth, made obsolete by globalization. He insists that collective entrepreneurship, the high-achieving team, needs time to develop so that members can appreciate each other's strengths, form close working relationships, break down functional silos, and redesign hierarchies. There is also a need for a new form of management – one of communication and coordination rather than command and control, with redesigned reward structures and more involvement in real decision making, because, as Reich comments:

"Underneath the veneer of participatory management, it is business as usual – and business as usual represents a threat to America's long-term capacity to compete."

This underestimation of staff has long been a subject for debate by writers on change, customer service, and excellence, and it is increasingly important in a world where competitive competency increasingly resides inside people's heads. This is one of the reasons that organizational learning has become such an important competency of so much management development activity. Individualism, which brings with it the desire to partition and protect knowledge, actively works against organizational learning and, by extension, organizational competitiveness. Firms are spending a great deal of money attempting to perfect their knowledge management systems, often through their IT systems, but what they are failing to develop is their human capital. Teams working together on problems learn how to solve them collectively and that knowledge remains embedded in the team. It might remain tacit knowledge and never be written down in a manual or posted to the intranet, but it is embedded in the organization.

Teamworking and organizational learning go hand in hand. A template for a successful firm might well be teams trying to outlearn each other rather than outperform each other on some arbitrary productivity scale. But this will only happen if reward systems are rethought. Credit needs to be given to the invisible work carried out by many team members which allows the group to function: the planning, scheduling, harmonizing activities which go on behind the scenes but which are not rewarded because they are largely invisible and pretty unexciting.

This leads on to some of the thinking inspired by the new science and the attention being paid to the role of the spirit at work. The spirituality of work is a whole new area for many managers and smacks a little of New Age thinking. Others are reluctant to engage with people's spirituality and religion for a variety of reasons. But one of the most moving writers on spirituality and work, Matthew Fox, states simply that if we start thinking about work as making a contribution our whole attitude will alter. Fox insists that people want to make a contribution, and this is highly relevant to teamworking. One person cannot make much of a difference, but when a team starts to perform, amazing things can happen. Even if the contribution is to developing a great team – doing the invisible work to make the team successful – the knock-on effects can be tremendous.

People interested in spirituality and work are also often interested in workgroups as communities, nurturing places where people can reach their highest potential. It is possible for communities to get stuck and for tensions within them to rip them apart, just as it is possible for what M. Scott Peck calls "pseudo communities" to develop, places in which conflict is suppressed and everyone smiles sweetly through gritted teeth. But when real communities emerge they ensure everyone's development both professionally and personally. Such communities are rare, but with the increasing popularity of Richard Greenleaf's servant leadership with many managers who see that supporting and developing people is better for everyone, including the organization as a whole, than command and control, it is possible that more communities will emerge. Peck writes:

> "Over the past 60 years, just as we've developed a technology that we can use to blow ourselves off the face of the earth, we've also very quietly and unknown to most people developed a technology we can use to make peace. . . . I call it community building."

Although very few people will recognize their organizations as communities, many will have worked in a team which was a real community where they felt valued, accepted, and respected. Having clear objectives is vital, but the desire to achieve them is enhanced by some of this community feeling.

The new science has many component parts but one of the most frequently used concepts is that of strange attractors, which comes from chaos theory. In the business context this is interpreted as a vision of something greater that draws people and their energy to it. In turn much of the writing applying such concepts to business often stresses that the universe is made up of relationships, the invisible glue keeping everything together. Jagdish Parikh writes:

> "The new physics asserts that the ultimate reality is a complex web of interrelationships, and intricate system of self-organizing, autonomous subsystems of energy fields. Therefore, to understand any part, we must understand the whole, the large systems of which it is a part. In this sense everything is interrelated – a

series of relationships within one vast relationship. Managing even one single relationship requires a deeper appreciation of the fundamental nature and interconnectedness, a unified theory, of all relationships."

Charles Handy describes organizations as containing "bundles of potentiality" which, seen in this light, need to be brought together into fruitful configurations or relationships. Parikh suggests that this is a difficult skill:

"It should be borne in mind that effectiveness in the relationship not only depends on the work-related relationship, but in fact, the work-related relationship itself will depend on the deeper level of person-to-person relationship. This is often overlooked. Therefore there is a lot of avoidable frustration because efforts focused mainly on the work-related relationship have not only not forged authentic relationships but frequently have led to manipulative and artificial relationships. Witness the persisting lack of mutual trust among workers at all levels despite the growing number of 'team-building' training sessions! That is not to say that such efforts or processes are undesirable – the point here is that these do not go far enough. Ultimately, any relationship will begin and depend on one's own relationship with all the 'dimensions' at the personal level – and this is often the main missing link."

It is, therefore, the personal as much as the strategic or the structural factors which make teams successful, and, as we have seen, effective teams will make an organization succeed.

TEAM LEADERSHIP

Teamworking, then, is of strategic importance to many organizations, but even in those where it is not seen in such elevated terms there is a need to get groups of people working together. Apart from odd articles describing team roles in terms of sitcoms or describing team-building games which may or may not add to organizational effectiveness, there are very few new insights into what makes teams work.

Probably the best-known book on teamworking is Katzenbach and Smith's *The Wisdom of Teams*, although, surprisingly, they are not single-minded advocates of teamwork. They make the distinction between teamworking and group working. Group working involves individuals working together to produce something, more for convenient access to resources than for synergy. Such workgroups have a single leader and their performance depends on the leader to delegate, monitor, intervene, and so on. Teamworking is qualitatively different, although not always preferable. Teamworking is not always warm and fuzzy; in fact these authors suggest that teamwork as a goal is a recipe for disaster and that "Teams are much more about discipline than togetherness." What marks out a team is a concentration on performance rather than the social aspects: " *the* single most powerful engine for teams is a clear and compelling performance challenge," and they add: "A hunger for performance is far more important to team success than team-building exercises, special incentives, or team leaders with ideal profiles."

Katzenbach and Smith give five insights into successful teaming:

» There are six team basics: teams should be small, fewer than 12 people; team members should have complementary skills; the team should have a common purpose; there should be a common set of specific purpose goals; there should be a commonly agreed working approach; there must be mutual accountability.
» A team approach should be chosen based on clearly defined performance outcomes. There must be a clear and compelling answer to the question, why do you need a team to achieve what you want to achieve?
» The team leader is seldom the primary determinant of team performance (having clear goals and a sense of purpose are far more likely to indicate success).
» Most organizations have enormous untapped potential for using teams.
» The organization needs a performance ethic or culture if it is to generate good teams.

In the revised edition of their book, Katzenbach and Smith list what they describe as "uncommonsense findings" about teams. These are:

» Companies with strong performance standards seem to spawn more "real teams" than companies that promote teams *per se*.
» High-performance teams are extremely rare.
» Hierarchy and teams go together almost as well as teams and performance (teams seem to be able to negotiate hierarchies and do not threaten them).
» Teams naturally integrate performance and learning (by defining goals and devising ways to meet them, then internalizing and replicating that knowledge).
» Teams are the primary unit of performance for increasing numbers of organizations (particularly to deliver responsiveness, speed, on-line customization, and quality).

Not everyone is so positive about teamworking. Frank Mueller and co-workers propose that successful teamworking happens along five dimensions which they label "TESCO," the name of a highly successful UK supermarket chain. These dimensions are:

» **Technological**: organizations need to think about production technology and task interdependence. Effective teamwork, particularly in the context of lean production, requires the intelligent use of production technology because the team can be dependent on the quality of materials and supply reliability. Bottlenecks and disruptions tend to force supervisors back into troubleshooting and disturbance-handling roles which mean that they end up back on the line thus undermining teamworking. High task interdependence is an important predictor of team success.
» **Economic**: teamworking will have an impact on performance which may initially be negative. Managers need to be prepared for this. In the longer term, multi-skilled teams will have an impact on cost, self-managing teams will have an impact on value, and self-led teams on innovation. One of the biggest economic problems is that of teamworking and reward. Finding a way to incentivize teams is particularly difficult. Should it be monetary or non-monetary? Should it involve a flat rate of some sort plus incentives? In which case, does this encourage people to coast along? Why is it so difficult for managers to shift away from individual incentives? What can be

done about the tremendous discomfort so many workers feel about managing their co-workers' performance?

» **Social**: good teams need to develop skills and competencies through training and development. There are two approaches to skilling the team: incremental or radical. Incremental development involves bringing in new talent and retaining an unequal division of labor at least in the short term. This is a problem if it leads to certain individuals cherry picking the most interesting tasks. Radical development is a longer-term option in that the team is not rolled out until everyone is equally skilled up. This is much more costly. Multi-skilling is still less common than specialization because it can be seen as costly and wasteful. Team members are also sometimes reluctant to lose their skills differentials and the pay structures that go with them.

» **Cultural**: one of the most common complaints about teamwork initiatives is that they are not matched by a change in management style. It is a paradox that many organizations claim that they want to use teams to improve creativity and innovation, but that teamworking can actually promote group think which can be as oppressive as overt management control. There are also problems with commitment to the team, particularly if an individual belongs to a number of teams. How many families can you be part of simultaneously?

» **Organizational and governance**: while organizations need to be structured around teams if they are to be successful it is difficult to make this work, particularly if there are powerful functional silos in existence. Transforming the team leader role from cop to coach is also difficult. Finding people with the right skills can be difficult, and teams seem unwilling to accept "outsiders." Finally, teamworking can sometimes be used against managers by wily teamworkers. If group performance is all important, why should people be subject to individual performance appraisal?

From this it can be seen that teamworking is open to abuse. It can be a way for managers to get workers to control themselves very closely, in effect putting themselves under surveillance. Thus it becomes a worker's rather than a manager's role to supervise.

There is a similar theme underpinning *Organizing Genius* written by Warren Bennis and Patricia Ward Biederman. Bennis has been a leading writer on leadership for many years, and in this book he and Biederman turn their attention to high-performing teams. They describe some leaders in less than complimentary terms in the book, implying that organizations do manipulate their workers for their own ends, but the description of the work of high-performing teams – what the authors call "great groups" – is highly seductive. Bennis and Biederman state that there are 15 "take home lessons" from the work of great groups, such as the early days at Apple Computers, the Disney feature animators, the Manhattan Project, and the team that got Clinton elected to the White House. These were groups that "made a dent in the universe" according to Steve Jobs' classic quotation. While not everyone feels that the work that their team does will make a similar dent, it is certainly a feeling worth aiming for.

The 15 points are:

» Great groups start with superb people. You need to recruit people who have the right skills but also the right temperament, and you should not be afraid to recruit people who are more intelligent than you!

» Great groups and great leaders create each other. There is something of a symbiotic relationship between the leader and the team: a great team can often create the conditions for its leader to come alive.

» Every great group has a strong leader. Although teams are blends of skills, there is often one person who is a real star, either because of their vision or some particular ability. One style of teamwork is that of the largely invisible group making space for a genius to work in. In the long term, however, that genius had better give something back to the team or they are likely to find themselves stranded.

» The leaders of great groups love talent and know where to find it. Sometimes this is a particular location; increasingly it is cyberspace. Great groups also stimulate or bring on home-grown talent as people excel in an effort to impress their peers.

» Great groups are full of talented people who can work together. This means creating a common way of working rather than necessarily getting on wonderfully well together – which may or may not be the case.

» Great groups think they are on a mission from God. Such groups think that their work is vital and they understand that it has real meaning. This is the oft-quoted example of medieval masons seeing their work as building cathedrals rather than cutting blocks of stone.

» Every great group is an island – but an island with a bridge to the mainland. Isolation can be physical or cultural – the group can be in an outpost of a multinational or in headquarters as long as it has something which makes it exclusive, such as in-jokes or customs.

» Great groups see themselves as winning underdogs. The parent organization is Goliath and the group is an energetic, dynamic David. Or Goliath is an industry which needs shaking up. Groups derive energy from going up against the big players.

» Great groups always have an enemy. Even if there is no enemy great groups create one.

» People in great groups have blinkers or blinders on. They fall in love with the project to the distraction of everything else, which can, of course, cause trouble in other areas of their lives.

» Great groups are optimistic, not realistic. In order to get things done great groups use the power of optimism not pessimism.

» In great groups the right person has the right job. This means that no one is too grand to do any particular task.

» The leaders of great groups give them what they need and free them from unnecessary detail. This involves providing people with the tools for the job. People in love with their work are often oblivious to their surroundings, but they do need access to equipment and other resources if they are to excel. They also need protection and sponsorship.

» Great groups ship. Great groups are productive. They do not simply design elegant products or think great thoughts. They solve problems and complete their tasks.

» Great work is its own reward. People in really great teams doing really important work often comment that they would go to work for nothing: the work itself is its own reward. The downside is that really great groups like this seldom last long; they burn themselves out.

KEY POINT

Teams are vital to organizations trying to leverage their core competencies; in fact some commentators would see teamworking itself as a critical capability. With the increased use of ICT teamworking will become more rather than less important, although the factors which make the best-performing teams are likely to remain in human hands rather than under technological control.

In Practice

» Wide selection of cases from Britain, the Unites States, and Asia, each with its key learning points.

KERRY FOODS

Kerry Foods delivers food products to a variety of retail outlets. This sounds simple enough until you realize that it is a strategic business unit formed after the Kerry Group, an Irish food products giant, bought up a number of smaller producers and merged the distribution services. There was the typical nightmare that follows a merger: how do we get different customs, practice, and culture to fit into one seamless whole? The tale continued to be familiar: different depots had the same vehicles, products, and procedures, but while some functioned well others produced a stream of complaints that the people back at head office had to deal with. There had to be something wrong with the corporate culture. Complaints, absenteeism, and staff turnover coupled with distrust of head office meant something had to be done. Sue Camm, the personnel and development manager, decided to undertake an audit of the company culture and turned to the University of Exeter to help her. They used a cultural audit tool called the Nine Key Factors survey which asks employees to rate their employer in terms of acceptance, fairness, respect, trust/agreement, expectations, balance, development, team spirit, and ownership. The returns showed that while employees in general rated the organization reasonably highly there were pockets of dissent and downright unhappiness.

So far so good. This case has a familiar ring. Where it is instructive is in what happened next. Instead of settling for a splashy article in the company magazine and a few staged quick wins, Kerry Foods managers decided to do something about the results. They refused the easy option of the quick-fix training event and went and listened to employees. There were some quick wins such as restoring the status of the van loaders (previously a bit inferior to the drivers) by giving them the symbolic Christmas hampers that the drivers only had previously received, but they also took seriously the feedback they received on their own style. Chumminess did not go down well with the people in the depots. And the familiar barriers between people who had worked for various companies prior to the merger were still standing. It called for a long-term solution including time-rich one-to-one meetings, training courses, and well-designed incentives. It also meant that area sales managers had to review their management styles and do something about them. Camm introduced the following initiatives:

» Weekly and annual performance incentives involving amounts that really meant something to the depot staff.
» Longer induction training and coaching.
» Staff working in smaller teams of three.

When the survey was repeated the following year the scores had risen consistently.

KEY LESSONS

» Expecting teamwork to follow on after a merger as night follows day is foolish.
» People retain their tribal loyalties long after the new logos have appeared on the letterheads.
» People have to be treated consistently if they are to work together and the culture of the organizational tribe needs to be established and nurtured if people are not to return to their local loyalties.

MINI-CASE: ENGLISH, WELSH, AND SCOTTISH RAILWAYS

EWS was experiencing major problems. It was in an industry sector which had been run down and was showing the signs. Even under new US management with promised reinvestment in rolling stock, the managing director, Ian Braybrook, realized that something fundamental would have to shift and focused his attention on a major culture change and restructuring employment conditions and working practices. As part of this program EWS targeted its team leaders, inviting them to undertake projects back in their workgroup. Some team leaders managed to save money by reducing waste and so on, but one innovative team leader kept a diary about developing himself and his team. He also sent out a questionnaire to find out what people thought of him as a manager. As a result productivity in the team went up 10-fold and everyone wanted to work in it.

KEY LESSONS

» Improving team spirit doesn't have to cost a fortune, but it does require investment.

» Teams respond to openness, honesty, and respect.

» Showing your vulnerable side, even in a macho industry like rail freight, will not necessarily get you killed.

» Cutting waste and rework is a quick win, but sustainable improvements are based on longer-term initiatives.

» Senior management can and should trust their teams to use their initiative to bring about improvements.

CONSOLIDATED DIESEL CO.

This is another story of what looks like an ordinary company making a fairly uninspiring product. It was formed in 1980 as a joint venture between Cummins Engine Co. and J.J. Case Corp. Consolidated Diesel is based in Whitakers, North Carolina, and has 1700 employees. The reason this story is interesting is that the company has a turnover rate of less than 2% and has never made a significant number of people redundant. The company attributes this to its life-long commitment to giving people an extraordinary level of responsibility and allowing them to figure out how to achieve an extraordinary level of productivity. The difference is shown in supervisor to staff ratios, traditionally around 1:25, which works out at a saving of about $1 million per year. At Consolidated Diesel it is 1:100. And the company can produce an engine in 72 seconds. People at the plant put this success down to teamworking and specifically to the socio-technical approach developed by the work of Trist and Bamforth with coal miners in the north of England in the 1950s (described in Chapter 3). This approach basically states that people know best how to do their jobs and how to organize their work and that if you listen to them and let them do it they will produce great results.

So, Consolidated Diesel concentrates on fairness and responsiveness. Either everyone gets a bonus or no one does. People rotate between day and night shifts. People are cross-trained so that they become multi-skilled and not deskilled (as was so clearly the case with the miners that Trist and Bamforth worked with). People are consulted and given authority to organize their own work schedules so that when business was slack it was the workers themselves who reduced shift length and suspended Saturday working. Because the plan was not a management imposition the teams made it work. And the managing director, Jim Lyons, really does walk the talk in a way that is so often recommended in management textbooks and training courses but so infrequently carried out. Instead of two huge 700-people briefings once a quarter, Lyons makes his state of the plant briefings to groups of 15. That way he gets more questions, and despite the fact that it is time consuming the changing tone of the questions assures him that his approach works. People are more likely to ask about plans for expansion than for closure.

KEY LESSONS

» Trust people and they will reward you.
» Trusting people is not only for nice white-collar and creative-type jobs. Empowerment works on the shop floor too.
» Teams will produce wisdom if you give them good information.
» Don't discard an idea just because it's old. Trist and Bamforth are as relevant in twenty-first-century manufacturing industry as they were in 1950s coal mines.

NATIONWIDE BUILDING SOCIETY CUSTOMER SERVICES DEPARTMENT

Building societies, which have traditionally provided savings and investment products alongside a core business of mortgage finance, are not usually thought of as exciting places to work. The time was, not so long ago, that you'd want your son or daughter to get a job in one for a nice, safe time and a meal ticket for life. As the sector has changed with many building societies transforming themselves into banks, so the working conditions have changed. The Nationwide realized early in the 1990s that it would have to change radically to compete. At the same time the annual staff satisfaction surveys showed the customer service part of the business only about half-way up the league tables in terms of employee satisfaction. It was time for decisive action. The customer services department needed to work within a flatter structure while continuing to develop a multi-skilling approach to its teams, and the idea of self-managing teams seemed to fit the bill. The project began in 1995 in an administrative center with 12 teams. They were given training in decision-making, conflict management, and team-building skills. The teams had between 9 and 18 members and a team leader who acted as a coach. As with the Consolidated Diesel experience responsibility for making decisions was delegated to the teams to make collectively, and here there was a slight competitive element added against the background culture that you are only as good as your worst-performing team.

This case is interesting because not everyone embraced their new-found autonomy. Some saw this as a way of getting them to do managerial work without getting the pay or prestige for it. Some team leaders saw the teams as a threat to their power and authority. Some were disheartened when the teams initially experienced a dip in performance. But shortly afterwards levels of performance began to pick up and attitudes began to change.

Along with performance, people's attitudes to their work began to change. Teams began to share their ideas with each other and to change their work processes. Team members took over responsibility for charting their own sickness and overtime figures and comparing those with other teams. Ownership of the numbers led to pride in improving them and the need for management intervention dwindled. Teams began to set up meetings with the front-line branch staff they supported and they began to examine ways that they could work to support each other and work together more efficiently.

The success at the first site encouraged the Nationwide to try out the self-managed team approach in other locations and operations including the human resources department. And this success is tangible and sustainable. Productivity in the customer services department increased by half, sickness absence fell by 75%, and overtime has been reduced to zero – an HR professional's dream come true! But the Nationwide is not complacent and has continued its training program, training staff in team skills so that they can take on new responsibilities. The emphasis is on team building and empowerment. There have been other implications: the success of the self-managed teams has meant a critical look at the structures that need to be in place to support teams and that implies some fundamental rethinking about the way the Nationwide organizes itself. What started as an initiative for one group in one function is having an impact on the whole business.

KEY LESSONS

» There needs to be a good business reason for introducing teams – not just because they are a current business fad. Are self-managed teams the best way to meet that business need or would one of what Katzenbach and Smith call a single-leader group be a better solution?

» There need to be measures in place from early on to chart the success of the team and a set of metrics that allow the team to monitor and improve its progress.

» Everyone needs to recognize that this is not a quick fix. There might be some short-term gains, but as Consolidated Diesel also shows, many of the gains only show up in the long term.

» There most definitely needs to be "buying in" on the part of employees likely to be involved in the process. Many people are suspicious of the motives behind teams and team incentives, even more so when these are self-managed teams. You need to have your answer ready when staff ask why they should take on the headaches of management without the pay.

MINI-CASE CLASSIC: HITACHI

In Japan, an "inside-the-company venture" was established at Hitachi in 1983. Earlier that year, Hitachi's president, Katsushige Mita, was approached by the managing director, Ozeki, and asked to create a special plant for office automation equipment "in order to make up for the company's serious delay in the field." Instead of looking at whether or not such a plant would be profitable, Mita said, "why don't you build a small shed and start from there as our predecessors did, when they founded the company?" Task groups and inside-the-company ventures are being used in companies throughout Japan. "We are trying to turn existing organizations into new venture units" says another company president (from *Ignition!* by Rani Chaudhry-Lawton and Richard Lawton).

KEY LESSONS
» Product innovation almost always needs a team to make it work.
» Organizations need to find ways to "chunk" themselves up if they are to react and respond to change. The strategic use of teams is a good way to do this.

CANON

Canon is one of the classic stories of strategy, along with Honda reinventing the motorcycle market in the United States. Canon's success in the photocopier market is always seen as a triumph for the RBV of strategic planning described in Chapter 6. Indeed, although the Canon success story, which began in the 1970s, is quite old now, it is still well worth thinking about in terms of how to leverage competencies to achieve competitive advantage.

In 1970 Xerox had a 93% share of the photocopier market. Like Hoover, its name had become a generic word for its product. Some people still talk about xeroxing a document. It looked like an invincible opponent, but within 20 years Canon had overtaken it in the number of units sold.

Many commentators looking at this example focus on the fact that Canon had very clearly defined competencies in fine optics, precision mechanics, electronics, and fine chemicals. Canon management also had an eye for a niche in a market. While Xerox went for large departmental machines, Canon decided to concentrate on smaller personal copiers. There was a gap in the market for these machines chiefly because no one thought that they were possible to make. Canon developed a machine and patented it and has enjoyed success with it ever since.

This sounds like classic strategic planning: decide what you want and are able to do, consider how your competitors might stop you, and do it. The tricky part is the last bit: doing it. There is no doubt that Canon has tremendous technical know-how, but it is also the case that the company knows how to mobilize that knowledge, and the way it does that is to mobilize teams at both the design and the manufacturing stages.

The company is committed to a decentralized research and design function and that necessarily means local teams. There are a number of product divisions each with its own development center which has a very clear vision of its task: to produce product designs and process improvement in the short to medium term. And, in textbook Japanese management style, most of the product development work is carried out by cross-functional teams. Then the work of these teams is coordinated by an R&D group located at head office.

Once a product goes into production, teams come to the fore again. The company operates a "stop and fix it" policy which empowers any worker to stop production if they cannot perform their function properly or they spot a quality problem. Most workers also participate in the "small-group activity" meetings for problem solving that we would call quality circles. So, work is organized through empowered self-managing teams who are responsible for quality and for continuous improvement. While Canon's senior management are proud of its technical expertise they also recognize that this is unlikely to guarantee sustained success without good management, and Canon provides a casebook example of how good management provides the environment for high-performing teams to flourish.

KEY LESSONS

» Japanese management techniques might have been a passing fad for many Western companies locked into the pursuit of short-term returns, but there is still a great deal to learn from the study of Japanese work methods.
» Teams are the best source of quality improvement gains.
» Innovation often comes from teams and organizations need to have structures to capture those insights.

MINI-CASE CLASSIC: SHARP CORPORATION

Sharp Corporation has used small groups to spearhead the company's new product development. Sharp has a special group of about 300 researchers, as well as 5000 engineers. The researchers are divided into subgroups of 10 people and each can freely select its members. No manager in the company can refuse requests from the leader of a subgroup. Each subgroup spearheads a new product development by taking full advantage of the company's human and other resources (from *Ignition!* by Rani Chaudhry-Lawton and Richard Lawton).

SOUTHWEST AIRLINES

Southwest Airlines is another strategy classic, this time as the story of a company that had a clear vision of its place in the market and therefore its core business and never, ever deviated from it. But the Southwest Airlines story is always more than that. This is an extraordinary company. Indeed, it attributes its enormous success in its particular segment of the market to what it calls "POS": Positively Outrageous Service. And, again, it acknowledges that it can only deliver that positively outrageous service through its highly trained, motivated, and committed service teams everywhere from booking to baggage handling.

A lot has been written about Southwest Airlines and its charismatic leader, Herb Kelleher, and one of the key features that emerges is the company's expert use of teams. The company has particularly flexible work rules and job descriptions which allow people to work in teams to get the job done. Sometimes these are official teams and sometimes they are temporary configurations of people who come together to solve a service problem. What the company promotes is a "whatever it takes mentality" which helps to break down demarcation lines based on status. At most airlines the pilots are a breed apart. They are so high up the food chain that they seldom seem to venture out of the cockpit. At Southwest, pilots see themselves as part of the team. They understand that a plane only makes money when it is in the air and that it is part of their job to get it there. So when there are delays Southwest pilots will help passengers in wheelchairs to board, help operations agents to take boarding cards, and help the flight attendants to clean up the cabin.

This desire to work as a team with the whole group of people who get the planes into the air, and therefore into profit, was the spur for the Cutting Edge Team project started by Cliff Slaughter, a Southwest captain. The project worked by getting a group of pilots to work on the ramps so that they could see what happened in and around the plane while it was at the gate. Pilots wore ramp agents' uniforms and the first shock was the way that they were treated by other people when they weren't in their own snappy uniforms. One described it as feeling like a second-class citizen. The value of the Cutting Edge Program, started by the original Cutting Edge Team, is that it gets people talking and breaks down barriers between them that become barriers to service. It does this by creating empathy. Literally, walking in other people's shoes sounds too simple and corny to be of any real help, but it allows multiple perspectives on problems and helps to develop a shared sense of history, both of which lead to improved customer service.

Southwest is also well known for the legendary speed of its turnaround of aircraft at the gate. Planes need to be flying to make money, not sitting at the gate and not losing slots. Southwest's customers are mainly business travelers going from city to city for work reasons and holiday makers visiting family in far-flung parts of the United States. The first group wants reliability and the second low prices. Only by keeping the planes in the air and full can Southwest deliver this and all its employees know it. Turnaround times have slowed down as airports have got bigger and the gates further from the runways, but it is still a team effort to get those planes off the tarmac and into the air so that they do not lose slots and therefore their reputation for reliability. And, as we have seen, everyone, including the captain, does their bit to ensure that that speedy turnaround takes place.

KEY LESSONS

» Being a team leader sometimes involves getting your hands dirty. This will not lead to loss of face as much as renewed faith from your team.
» Great teamwork is built on great training and great communication.

> » Teams will spontaneously come up with creative ways of making improvements if you just let them.

MINI-CASE CLASSIC: PRINCESS DIANA'S WEDDING SLIPPERS MAKER

Twenty years ago Clive Shilton was commissioned to make Lady Diana Spencer's wedding slippers. He was so nervous that something might go wrong and damage the shoes that he made two identical pairs. While he did the designing himself, he and his partner made sure that their team of eight people all had a hand in making the shoes for the historic event. And Shilton's team really did involve everyone. He said in a recent interview: "Even the cleaner banged a tack in. That way everyone could say that they had helped to make her wedding shoes."

KEY LESSON

> » Inclusion is a key feature in teamwork. If someone feels left out or like a second-class citizen they are unlikely to do their best work. Consideration costs very little but is likely to have a disproportionate effect on morale and productivity. The best managers and team leaders instinctively understand this, but even those of a low emotional IQ can take steps to improve it.

HEATHROW EXPRESS CONSTRUCTION PROJECT

It is now possible to get to London's Heathrow airport from Paddington Station using the smooth, fast, direct Heathrow Link, but at one stage the project looked as if it were heading for disaster. On Friday October 21, 1994, a landslip led to the partial collapse of three parallel tunnels being constructed as part of the link under the airport's central terminal area. Concrete had to be poured into the freshly dug tunnels to stop further collapse and the temporary housing for the workers had to be pulled down.

BAA (British Airports Authority), the developer, faced huge problems. No one had been killed or injured, but there would inevitably be an official health and safety inquiry, the very tunneling methods used would come under scrutiny, and costs would rise significantly above the original £300 million estimate. In the event the Health and Safety Executive did allow the construction methods to continue but the opening of the link was delayed.

The construction industry is known to be combative and litigious and the usual approach would be for the partners to start blaming each other. For once, BAA and BICC, which owns Balfour Beatty, the constructor, decided to look for a more constructive solution. They split the costs of the disaster, and, in an innovative move, set up a "solutions team." This team involved BAA, Balfour Beatty, and the other main contractors to sort out the technical problems – in effect a multi-agency, cross-functional problem-solving team. Chris Rust D'Eye was then appointed as the project's construction director. He too brought a fresh approach to the problem and also insisted on using teamworking as part of the solution. He instigated a major training program for the staff involved in the project and he also formed a "single team." This replaced the supervisory group that BAA would normally set up. It had members from all the major suppliers and it had a clear common goal: to open the link on time and without further safety problems. A further spin-off would be financial savings made by combining roles and sharing responsibility for much of the managerial work. People from different companies moved into the same building to allow them to communicate and share ideas.

Some counter-cultural elements began to creep in, such as workshops in which people worked on issues rather than holding meetings with fixed agendas, and contractual letters (specifying standards and expectations) were replaced with open discussion leading to agreements which were minuted. Open meetings were held with suppliers, which were informal events encouraging people to talk to each other. Front-line staff and contract and temporary staff were included to an unusual degree and were eligible for extensive training. All this cost money, but BAA considered that the single-team initiative saved £1.5 million often through reducing duplication. Because the single team could, for example, use 10 surveyors instead of the estimated 20, £400,000 was saved in one fell swoop.

The project has been so successful that BAA is considering introducing a similar approach elsewhere in its business. But one of the major benefits has been the reduction of suspicion in a traditionally fairly confrontational sector. As people began to see progress emerging from the single team their suspicions diminished and their trust and motivation grew. Then they were prepared to support the initiative and a virtuous circle was born.

KEY LESSONS

» It's easy to think that teams are just for front-liners but even senior managers can see benefits from concerted team efforts.
» Several heads with a single, very clear vision really can make huge returns.
» Teams can be counter-cultural and bring about more than productivity gains.
» A team leader with vision can make teams work even in seemingly inhospitable environments.

THE MAYO CLINIC

While the Mayo Clinic might not be a household name in Britain, it has an 85% name recognition rating in the United States. In common with the Heathrow Express Construction Project it operates in a counter-cultural way which sounds perfectly reasonable to the general public if not to its own professional bodies. The Mayo Clinic has its origins in a clinic opened in Minnesota by William Worrall Mayo in 1859. The philosophy of the founding father is still apparent in the way the clinic and its other facilities in the United States run today. Mayo insisted that the best interests of the patient should come before everything else and this ethos is continued in the present-day staff's approach to medicine. Essentially what makes the Mayo clinic distinctive is that patient care is based on teamwork. Instead of patients being ascribed to one particular doctor, they are the center of a specially constituted team, potentially different for each patient. The patients themselves also form part of the team, although how big a contribution they make depends on the patient. Some patients want to be told what to do, others, and this is increasingly the case, want to take a more active role in their care.

The team-based approach means that the patient is surrounded by team members who work in a way that is very similar to problem-based learning. The team is driven by a medical problem which needs to be solved and it might contract or expand to come up with a solution which is consistent with the patient's preferences. The team works on diagnosis and proposing a solution and then on the administration for ensuring that the treatment is carried out.

Given that medicine continues to be a hierarchical profession, this is a counter-cultural way to work. Doctors' decisions can be overturned by other members of the team who might have expertise leading to a different diagnosis or procedure. They also have to take account of what the patient wants and they know that their work will be closely examined by their peers. Good doctors obviously relish this opportunity to develop their skills and to continue their own learning, but for those who stand on ceremony, working at the Mayo is probably not a good career choice. This team approach is instilled from day 1 when new recruits are expected to join a number of committees which run the Mayo's various facilities through various collaborative decision-making structures. Furthermore, medicine has become big business with doctors competing for patients and contracts. The Mayo Clinic does not have any financial incentives which encourage competition. Doctors receive a fixed fee which is part of the culture that encourages collaboration. This collective approach stems directly from William Worrall Mayo's advice to his sons that "No one is big enough to be independent of others."

KEY LESSONS

» Even in a hierarchical, conservative profession teamwork can succeed and produce great results.

» Teamwork needs to be built into all the activities of an organization if it is to have a full impact on its culture.

- Money needs to follow teamwork. In this example there is an audaciously counter-culture level pay structure; in other cases there need to be team incentives.
- The customer is part of the team. This must be one of the most clichéd pieces of business advice, and one which is most often given lip service, but the Mayo example shows that even in a traditional we-know-best expert culture it is vital to include your customers as partners rather than adversaries.

Key Concepts and Thinkers

Approximately 500-word entries on major related concepts and thinkers.

MEREDITH BELBIN AND TEAM TYPES

Belbin's team types are extremely well known and form the basis of a great deal of team-building exercises. Belbin began to work on high-performing teams when he was working at Henley Management College. He began to get interested in how to predict what would make a good team into an excellent team. He devised a game which he ran with different groups of practicing managers over nine years and observed that most people have a preferred way of working in groups which he called their team type. These were based on personality traits and orientations which form a continuum (Fig. 8.1).

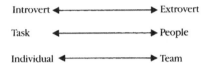

Fig. 8.1

Belbin developed a self-administered questionnaire or inventory which allowed people to work out their team type, and to develop their strengths by working on their preferred style and their weaknesses by working on their least favorite style.

A really effective group, according to Belbin, has a representative of each of the team types. There are nine team roles and where there is a smaller team Belbin suggests that people should develop their secondary role, that is their second favorite team type, to redress the balance. The team types are:

» **Plant**: this is the ideas person who might be "planted" in a sluggish group to shake them up a bit and get them working more creatively. The plant is probably best characterized by the stereotype of the absent-minded, eccentric genius who lives in a world of their own, dreaming up schemes which others might have to turn into a reality. They can be arrogant and unapproachable and have no regard for time or petty rules. But they can also be a breath of fresh air, and able to solve complex problems.

» **Resource investigator**: this is the person who can't answer your question but always knows someone who can. Or can't provide you with some particular resource but knows where they can get one cheaply. They have large networks of contacts and are seldom at their desks, or, if they are, they are e-mailing someone somewhere about something. They are usually warm, friendly, positive, and optimistic. They love putting people together and making connections, but they have limited attention spans and sometimes tend to be uncritical of the latest person, thing, or idea.

» **Coordinator**: this tends to be the person who focuses on the group's objectives and puts the wheels in motion so that they are met. These people often have a natural air of authority and inspire confidence. They listen to others and take all views into account. They can lead a team without being the official leader. Although they inspire loyalty they aren't always the brightest member of the team.

» **Shaper**: these people make things happen. They love to be in control. They love the adrenaline rush of a crisis. They want results and will push people to get them. They are highly dynamic and characterized by their drive and energy. They love to shake people up. All this means that they are likely to achieve results but they can topple over into bullying and frightening people.

» **Monitor–evaluator**: these people are quite rare. They come across as a bit reserved and distant. You could work with them for years and not really know them as they tend to keep their emotions to themselves. They weigh up the pros and cons of ideas. They monitor progress and make sure that the i's have been dotted and the t's crossed. They stop teams committing themselves to bad and hasty decisions. But they can really put the damper on things and there will probably not be a rush to sit next to them at the Christmas dinner.

» **Teamworker**: these people are good to have around. They are team players. They get on with the work. They like people and people like them. They are constructive rather than critical, and they understand people, and help to diffuse conflict. They are good for team spirit. Their main problem is that they adapt to change rather than initiating it, and they can be indecisive in a crisis.

» **Implementer**: every team needs an implementer or two to put ideas into practice, and to plan how to get the team to meet its objectives. They will get on with a job whether they enjoy it or not, having great loyalty to the organization and its objectives. They love systems, procedures, and budgets. They have natural organizational abilities and bags of common sense. But because they have so much common sense they can be a bit inflexible and plodding and resistant to change.

» **Completer**: these people believe that standards really matter. Perfection is just about good enough. They do things painstakingly thoroughly with an eye for detail, and they get them done on time. They are extremely irritated by slapdash work or any sense they might get that people are not taking their work seriously. They are conscientious, worry about their work, and are often obsessively neat. They also worry non-stop, and find it difficult to delegate to others.

» **Specialist**: increasingly teams need specialists with their own areas of knowledge which they love to hone and develop. There can be problems because they can be completely uninterested in anyone else's work and they can find it difficult to understand other people's problems. On the other hand they make good decisions based on their own expert knowledge and they are single-minded and proactive in their own areas.

There are other sets of team types such as solver, doer, checker, carer, and knower, but Belbin is probably the best known and most widely used.

Belbin's critics point to the fact that this is a self-administered questionnaire and therefore has limited validity, while others question the pigeonholing of people into these categories. At the very least the inventory can form the basis of interesting team development sessions.

WILFRED BION AND THE UNCONSCIOUS LIFE OF GROUPS

This is one very particular explanation of the age-old problem of why some groups work and some groups fail. Bion was one of the first people to argue in a systematic way that while there is an observable life of a group – one that can be seen in what people do – there is another level in existence, the psychological life of the group which has its reality in people's unconscious. The unconscious mind makes people do things which appear absolutely incomprehensible but make perfect sense at some deeper psychological level. An example of this is people sabotaging a project because at an unconscious level they know that its completion would mean the disbanding of a team which has come to be like a family to them. Thus, what looks like a complete contradiction to their best interests is logical when seen from this perspective.

Bion was greatly influenced by the work of theorists of the unconscious such as Freud. He carried out his research working with military patients during World War II, and concluded that there is a certain commonality in group experience; that is, there are certain patterns of behavior that all groups reproduce. He believed that there are two modes of group working. The first is work mentality in which people work on the task in hand. These groups are functional and work well. Then there are dysfunctional groups which are trying to avoid doing the task, as in the sabotage example above, and Bion called these basic assumption groups. Bion argued that basic assumption groups are characterized by anxiety. Sometimes that is just the scariness of life itself (particularly acute in combat) but often the anxiety is over fear of the boss, fear of looking stupid, fear that the task is beyond you, fear that you will be found out, and so on. Bion concluded that groups develop a range of behaviors to deal with these fears. These are:

» Dependency groups where the members look for a strong leader (not necessarily the official team leader) to deal with their fears for them to the exclusion of the talents and skills of other group leaders. Dependency can be on rituals and habits as well as people (let's just go round the room and see what everyone thinks, let's just jot a few things down on a flip chart, etc., instead of making a decision). This leads to blocked creativity and an inability to learn or change. This kind of group cannot function without its leader.

» Pairing groups are groups where a group allows two members to deal with its anxiety for it. This can take the form of two people slugging it out in an argument or two people flirting, to jokes about two stags locking antlers. The important thing is that the rest of the group stays out of it and watches. Again this blocks the contributions of the rest of the group.

» Fight or flight groups are groups in which either conflict is ignored altogether and everyone maintains a falsely bright atmosphere, or conflict is open and people bicker and argue about details instead of discussing what is really upsetting them.

Bion's method was to confront these behaviors and make people aware of when they were acting in a dysfunctional way. This has much in common with process consultation in which consultants comment on the way a group is behaving, its process, rather than putting anything into the content of a meeting. Bion believed that groups could switch very rapidly between being workgroups and basic assumption groups, and this is often seen in meetings where the atmosphere can change very quickly.

Although many people like to denigrate these kinds of theories, arguing that they are team leaders or managers and not psychiatrists, those who are open to such ideas often find that intractable problems are solvable if approached from this angle.

One of the contemporary writers on groups who is very much in this tradition is Larry Hirschhorn.

GROUP DEVELOPMENT

Anyone who has led a group over a period of time will have noticed that groups go through distinct stages. There are often fights at the beginning before people settle down to working together. There are a number of frameworks which propose how this works, the best known of which is probably B. Tuckman's four-stage forming, storming, norming, and performing sequence:

» **Forming**: the group are a bit uncertain and anxious about what they are supposed to be doing. They are concerned with issues of orientation and finding out what their objectives and various roles are to be. At this point they often test the boundaries of the group, and, in particular, question the authority of the leadership.
» **Storming**: the group's tensions and rivalries begin to surface. There is likely to be conflict and polarization around interpersonal issues.
» **Norming**: the group establish some cohesion which makes it possible for people to express their opinions. Group rituals, in-jokes, and ways of doing things are also likely to be established at this stage.

» **Performing**: the group finally reach a stage where they can focus on the task. Group structure has been sorted out and people are free to contribute to the achievement of their tasks. People are also ready and able to take on functional, flexible tasks.

People sometimes add further stages to the group formation sequence such as "mourning" when the group break up. Again this sequence is so familiar to people from such a number of training courses that it can be dismissed as corny or hackneyed, but it is a valuable tool for a team leader confused by sudden outbreaks of arguments or people trying to undermine the authority of others. There are other development frameworks such as I. Yalom's orientation, conflict, and cohesiveness, but Tuckman's has the benefits of being short, easy to understand, and memorable. Most group development frameworks, however, stress that one of the crucial points of the life of a group or team is when a member leaves or a new person joins. Often the team has to repeat the whole sequence, and sometimes the loss of a key member can unbalance the team to such an extent that it never recovers and ultimately breaks up.

DAVID MERRIL'S TEAM PROFILES

Merril is not as well known as Belbin, but he also sees people taking on certain roles in organizations according to their personality types. He also sees behavior along a continuum, but this time there are two sets of behaviors forming a 2 × 2 grid, as shown in Fig. 8.2.

People in teams fit into these zones in the way shown in Table 8.1.

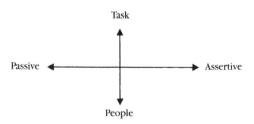

Fig. 8.2

Table 8.1

Analytical	Drivers
Perfectionists, love rules and models, love data and numbers. Not very keen on people or emotions What matters: doing things right	Love making things happen. Leaders, entrepreneurs, motivators. Can be absolutely terrifying. Expect results from everyone, including themselves What matters: getting results
Amiable	*Expressive*
Good, nice team people who care about others. Cooperative and inclusive. Seek harmony and consensus. Are people persons What matters: everyone is happy	Love to be stars. Want to be the center of attention. Creative, flamboyant, unusual. Lots of ideas, lots of contacts. Great networkers. Lots of stories and anecdotes What matters: getting attention

As with Belbin, it is possible to question a framework which claims that entire populations may be fitted into four boxes, but, in use, the discussion of these categories allows people an insight into why they find it so difficult to work with certain people, particularly those in boxes which are diametrically opposed to their own.

TEAM LEADERSHIP

There is little difference between team and other forms of leadership. Essentially good team leadership revolves around treating people as you would like to be treated yourself and leading people in the way that they would like to be led. So good team leadership is characterized by Ros Jay, for example, as requiring:

» Integrity – you should mean what you say and act consistently. You should give credit where it is due and not try to keep the praise and pass on the blame. You should treat everyone equally and not make promises that you cannot keep.

» Being positive – moaning bosses are a nightmare, as are bosses who blame "the people at head office" for unpleasant decisions. Being positive is one of the best ways of motivating people in times of crisis.
» Being likeable – there is a received idea somewhere in our culture that the best way to get people to do things is to shout at them, and that the hallmark of a great leader is respect. It is true that bullying tactics can have a short-term payoff, but for a team to perform excellently over a long period of time requires a gentler touch. People work harder for those they like.
» Being polite – there is no doubt that the small acts of saying "please" and "thank you" to team members increases their loyalty and therefore your chances of being a successful leader.
» Generosity – give and take. People respond to being treated like human beings and so if you can make a few allowances for off-days, or work something out to allow carers some flexibility, you should. Again you will be repaid by people's loyalty.

A highly influential figure in the debate about management is Ken Blanchard, the creator of the One Minute Manager series. Blanchard argues that leadership depends on the followers and that there is no one single best way of leading. He suggests that managerial activities are divided into directive behavior:

> "Clearly telling people what to do, how to do it, where to do it, and when to do it, and then closely supervising their performance."

And supportive behavior:

> "Listening to people, providing support and encouragement for their efforts, and then facilitating their involvement in problem-solving and decision-making."

He considers that it is the leader's job to assess the level of maturity of the follower and match the mix of directing and supporting to that individual's needs. He assesses maturity according to the person's competence and commitment. Competence is:

"a function of knowledge and skills, which can be gained from education, training and/or experience"

whereas commitment is:

"a combination of confidence and motivation. Confidence is a measure of a person's self-assuredness – a feeling of being able to do a task well without much supervision, whereas motivation is a person's interest in and enthusiasm for doing a task well."

So a good leader will treat a star performer who knows exactly what they are doing very differently from a new joiner who needs a great deal of the sort of direction that a star performer would see as interference. This scheme makes sense, but it requires good diagnostic skills on the part of the leader and some understanding on the part of the followers. Star performers, for example, might want more attention than Blanchard's framework allows. From the point of view of the team this approach is interesting because it suggests that the team leader's relationship to it will change over time. As the team develops through its forming, storming, norming, and performing phases the leader can be less and less directive. Blanchard also states, however, that new projects and responsibilities can turn star performers into beginners again and the shrewd team leader will take this into account in a group's performance.

Other important developments in recent thinking for team leaders have been the growth of self-managed teams and the emergence of servant leadership. Self-managed teams are groups of people empowered to make their own decisions and plan their own work. Many team leaders and supervisors are anxious about this idea because it suggests that they will become superfluous, but the evidence seems to suggest that where self-managed teams work well the leader's job is rotated around the group and the designated leader is freed up to do more interesting work. Thus the leader becomes a coach or facilitator to the group. Leaders who do not like this role unfortunately sometimes feel they have to leave the organization or go back to a more hands-on role, but others discover that they find their new way of working more satisfying.

Servant leadership, developed by Robert Greenleaf, works with the idea that far from commanding and controlling groups, the best leaders are at the service of their followers, enabling them to do good work and to develop to their fullest potential. This is linked to the idea that work can have a spiritual quality, which was discussed in Chapter 6. Although critics often take a cynical view of Greenleaf's work, seeing it as being too "touchy-feely," many leaders describe the best part of their jobs as seeing people develop and take on things that they would never have thought possible.

Resources

- » Easy reference to everything covered in the book.
- » Suggestions for further reading.
- » Useful Websites.

BOOKS AND ARTICLES

A great deal has been written on teams and teamworking. Here is a selection of books and articles, including several classics, which will give a grounding in the subject while avoiding some of the repetition. It also shows you where to get information on all the sources mentioned in this book.

Patricia J. Addesso (1996) *Management would be easy... if it weren't for the people*. Amacom, New York

Useful book on the difficulties of bringing together disparate groups of people to perform a number of tasks.

R. Meredith Belbin (1981, 1998) *Management Teams: Why They Succeed or Fail*. Butterworth–Heinemann, Oxford

One of the best-known and most widely used team-type inventories. So well known that it is sometimes dismissed as old hat and criticized for its tendency toward universalizing people's experience, it contains a useful starting point, at least, for getting people to talk about their preferred way of working and their experience in teams. Suggests that teams are best made up of people who together can fulfill a number of specific roles.

Warren Bennis and Patricia Ward Biederman (1997) *Organizing Genius: The Secrets of Creative Collaboration*. Nicholas Brearley, London

Bennis usually writes about leadership, but here turns his attention to the led. He can't quite resist writing about charismatic leaders, but deals with a series of case studies of very high-performing teams: Disney, Apple, Clinton's election team, Lockheed Skunk Works, Black Mountain College, and the Manhattan Project. From this, the authors distill a series of 15 take-home lessons on how to create great teams. Although the book deals with groups who feel that they are making a dent in the universe, to borrow Steve Jobs' phrase, it is a particularly interesting book and many of the lessons can be translated into much less glamorous team settings.

Wilfred Bion (1961) *Experiences in Groups.* Tavistock, London

Great British theorist of the unconscious life of groups and how this impacts on their ability to achieve their tasks. Probably not a book for a beach holiday.

Ken Blanchard (1995) *Leadership and the One Minute Manager.* HarperCollins Business, London

One of the best-known popular writers on business and management turns his attention to leading a team. The book contains a useful framework for getting the most out of individuals to lead to the development of a flourishing team.

Rick Brinkman and Rick Kirschner (1994) *Dealing with People You Can't Stand: How to Bring Out the Best in People at Their Worst.* McGraw-Hill, New York

A book about difficult people in general, but with a great section on what really matters to various team types which is genuinely useful in sorting out communication breakdowns in teams in trouble.

David Butcher and Catherine Bailey (2000) "Crewed awakenings." *People Management*, 3 August

Takes a hard look at the disillusion many organizations feel about their teamworking initiatives. They conclude that although the cherished aims are worthwhile they are no longer totally relevant given that people increasingly work on a more contingent basis. They move on to a consideration of virtual teams and make sensible recommendations about how to make them work.

Rani Chaudhry-Lawton and Richard Lawton (1991) *Ignition! Sparking Organizational Change.* Century Business, London

Not specifically on teams, but gives lots of classic cases of where small groups have been vital to producing creativity, innovation, and corporate renewal.

Soumitra Dutta and Arnoud De Meyer (1997) "Knowledge management at Arthur Andersen (Denmark): building assets in real time and in virtual space." INSEAD, ECCH case 397-00-1

Good example of the impact of new technology on teamworking based on Arthur Andersen's Danish branch.

Joyce Fletcher (1999) *Disappearing Acts*. MIT Press, Cambridge, MA

Challenging book on the way we ignore the invisible work that keeps teams functioning and the insidious way that individualism works against teamwork and personal development in general.

Matthew Fox (1994) *The Reinvention of Work: A New Vision of Livelihood for Our Time*. Harper, San Francisco

Beautifully written book with a compelling vision of what work could be like if it were reconceptualized as making a contribution. One of the influential books on seeing organizations as nurturing communities.

Kevin and Jackie Freiberg (1998) *Nuts! Southwest Airlines' crazy recipe for business and personal success*. Broadway, New York

A pacy and engaging biography of a company famous for its levels of service. The whole book is full of examples of the transformational nature of truly effective teamwork. The breathlessly admiring style of the writers gets a little cloying after a while, but only the most hard-bitten corporate cynic could fail to be impressed by the letters from customers and testimonies from employees. A counter to the argument that whole organizations cannot be teams.

John Grundy and Jennifer Ginger (1998) "Global teams for the millennium." *Management Decision*, 36 (1)

Good introduction to the impact of globalization on teams and team-working using the offshore drilling industry. Suggests that a move toward virtual teaming is inevitable.

Colin Hastings, Peter Bixby, and Rani Chaudhry-Lawton (1994) *Superteams: Building Organizational Success through High Performing Teams.* AMED, London

Good solid introduction to leading teams and using them well in your organization.

Larry Hirschhorn (1991) *Managing in the New Team Environment: Skills, Tools and Methods.* Addison-Wesley, London

Firmly rooted in the psychological school of management thinking, this book aims to make theories about the hidden, unconscious drivers of people in teams accessible to practicing managers. Although the material presented is dense and complex, Hirschhorn concentrates on helping managers to diagnose the deep dysfunctions in their teams and gives many case examples of how problems might be overcome.

Geert Hofstede (1991) *Cultures and Organizations: Intercultural Cooperation and its Importance for Survival.* McGraw-Hill, London

Systematic study of differences in culture across the global network of IBM. May be criticized for its small sample size and dependence on one company, but a useful starting point for thinking about the impact of globalization on teamworking.

Ros Jay (2000) *Build a Great Team: Choose the Right People for the Right Roles.* Prentice Hall, London

Based quite heavily on Belbin's team types, this book is very much about the human side of leading a team and concentrates on the necessary processes for team building such as running team meetings, interviewing, appraisals, and so on. A good introduction to Belbin and a nice counterbalance to some of the hard-headed teams by objective writing.

Geraint John (1998) "Twist of freight." *People Management*, 12 November

Instructive case study on introducing teamworking in a traditionally conservative environment. Tackles the issue of people's suspicion of teamwork initiatives.

Jon R. Katzenbach and Douglas K. Smith (1993, 1999) *The Wisdom of Teams: Creating the High-performance Organization*. HarperCollins Business, New York

Probably the most influential book on teams and teaming around – the one essential book to have on your bookshelf. Based on years of experience, this book takes a very firm line on the need to establish a clear set of objectives for teams and to be very sure that teamwork is what is needed to achieve them. Has extensive case studies and clearly set-out learning points. Particularly interesting to hear about the difficulty of getting senior managers to work in teams, and to overcome the individualism in Western society when aiming for collectivism from writers from the McKinsey consulting house.

David Littlefield (1999) "Kerry's heroes." *People Management*, 6 May

Useful case study on making a merger work through planned and thoughtful use of teams. Instructive on the need to follow through to create the culture necessary for teams to flourish.

Frank Mueller, Stephen Proctor, and David Buchanan (2000) "Teamworking in its context(s): antecedents, nature and dimensions." *Human Relations*, 53 (11)

Scholarly article on the history of teamworking which repays a careful reading.

Jagdish Parikh (1999) *Managing Relationships*. Capstone, Oxford

One of the more accessible books on the connection between the new science and the world of work. Stresses the importance of relationships as the organizing principle of the universe which is of direct relevance to teams and teamworking in organizations.

Donald Petersen and John Hillkirk (1991) *Teamwork: New Management Ideas for the Nineties*. Gollancz, London

Although this is a bit old now, it gives a fascinating insight into the dilemmas facing a senior management team at a very large company, in this case the Ford Motor Company. It is an extended case study, based on Petersen's experience as CEO at Ford, and gives an insider's view of famous cases such as the development of the Taurus. Engaging for the hint of surprise that the Europeans can do something better than Americans, in this case collaborative teamworking.

Harvey Robbins and Michael Finley (1996) *Why Teams Don't Work: What went wrong and how to make it right*. Orion Business Paperbacks, London

An award-winning book which concentrates on the obstacles to high performance in teams. It is an engaging read, distinguishing, for example, between mobs and teams, and identifying team types such as team jerks, dark angels, and team brats, but readers might find the full-on pally style heavy going after 200 pages. Contains a great many pieces of useful advice with the ring of truth about them, and checklists for dealing with ailing teams.

Paul Roberts (1999) "The agenda – total teamwork." *Fast Company*, April

Compelling case study of how an organization can develop and sustain a team culture in a sector which is traditionally characterized by individualism and status. Considers the history and success of the Mayo Clinic, and suggests that rapid change is not always the best way to succeed.

Warren Scott and Hilary Harrison (1997) "Full team ahead." *People Management*, 9 October

Case study which shows how the sensitive implementation of teamworking can completely transform levels of morale and motivation.

Curtis Sittenfield (1999) "Power by the people." *Fast Company*, July/August

Compelling case example of the long-term benefits of using self-managed teams in an engineering context. Illustrates the importance of a visionary and committed leader. Useful example of a company where the ideas have been in use for many years.

Mike Thatcher (1997) "Digging for victory." *People Management*, 6 November

Impressive case study of counter-cultural teamwork initiative at the Heathrow Express Construction Project.

B. Tuckman (1965) "Development sequences in small groups." *Psychological Bulletin*, 63, 384–99

It's unlikely that many people would track this down, but if they did they might be surprised to discover that the famous forming, storming, norming, and performing sequence is included almost as an afterthought in the final pages of a pretty scholarly article. Similarly, very few people will want to seek out I. Yalom's *The Theory and Practice of Group Psychotherapy* (Basic Books, New York, 1970), although his orientation, conflict, cohesiveness framework is shorter, if not as catchy as Tuckman's.

USEFUL WEBSITES

Most Websites on teams and team building tend to offer training workshops or pyramid selling opportunities. The following three, however, offer a wealth of information and are worth an occasional look.

www.workteams.unt.edu

Website of the Center for the Study of Work Teams. Offers a vast resource of current research.

www.trainingzone.co.uk

Features provocative articles on a range of management subjects including an interesting look at the realities of teamwork for senior managers.

www.bestofbiz.com

Interesting material on the 21st Century team from the London Business School.

Ten Steps to Making it Work

» Distilled wisdom of writers on teams, case studies, and interviews.
» Practical advice on how to make teams work and how to have realistic expectations of what they can produce.

As we have seen, there is a wealth of experience of making teams effective in organizations. Here we distill the best of current wisdom.

1. DECIDE IF YOU REALLY NEED A TEAM

This sounds slightly bizarre in a book on teamwork, but one of the crucial questions that any organization considering teamworking needs to ask itself is: "Do we really need a team? Might we be better off with workgroups?" The distinction is subtle. Workgroups look like teams but they are made up of individuals with a single leader who makes the decisions and runs the show. Teams are made up of interdependent people who could not achieve their objectives separately. So you need to decide whether you want to make the investment in making your team work, or whether it would be better to organize as groups.

You might want a team if you want high-quality problem solving, increased creativity and innovation, or great knowledge management. Teams are a wonderful way of capturing and operationalizing organizational learning. They are a great way of blending individuals' specialist skills and achieving the synergy that comes from putting a talented group of people together to make something, to decide on something, or to manage something. It sounds wonderful. But, teams need a lot of work and a willingness to look to the long term. They are never a short-term fix.

When you do get your team up and running it will be a great experience for everyone involved and that will bring with it another set of concerns. Exactly who will you let into your team? Does it have fixed membership or is it open to everyone? Given that the ideal team probably has no more than 12 members you will probably need an entry policy, but once a team starts to be successful people are likely to want to join it, so be prepared. And think about what will happen when the team has met its objectives and the time comes to wind it up. You may need to be firm if being on the team is one of the main sources of motivation for your people.

2. DO YOU HAVE THE ORGANIZATIONAL CULTURE TO MAKE TEAMS WORK?

Making teams work is not just about everyone being nice to each other. Again it requires planning. Do you have a reward structure in place to make team rather than individual performance a well-motivated activity? Does your whole corporate culture favor macho heroics or a supportive, developmental approach to creating groups of people with common aims? Are you good at defining your objectives? Will your team know exactly what it is and is not supposed to be doing? Do your senior managers ever work as a team? What are they role-modelling? Cooperative working or turf battles and points scoring? Do you have the atmosphere of trust that is needed to make virtual and actual teams work or do you like to keep a close eye on things? Are you willing to shift what you are doing and the ways you work if a team culture really takes off? Building your activities around teamworking is not to be entered into lightly!

3. HOW WELL DO YOU COMMUNICATE?

Whenever I ask a group of managers what they think contributes to the effectiveness of teamworking the same answer always comes up: communication. We hear a lot about communication to the point where it seems to be the answer to every organizational problem, but with teamworking it really is vital. A group of people unable to share information are unlikely to achieve their aim. Communication in this case is not just about passing on information – although that is important and no team can function without the data it needs to do its job – it is about a commitment to treating people like adults. Communication goes hand in hand with trust and integrity. People like to be included as much as possible and this means telling them as much as you can that isn't commercially sensitive. It is quite difficult to over-communicate. Over the years a number of managers have told me that they don't want to pass on bad news in case it upsets their staff. The reality is that in the absence of information people make things up that are far worse, and teams have a ready-made structure and opportunity for doing it. Finally on this point, it is possible to say one thing to your team with your words and quite another with your actions. Telling your team that there is a no-blame culture and that mistakes are challenges and opportunities for learning will cut little ice if you then shout at people and conduct witch-hunts. The content and the process of communication needs to be robust.

4. HAVE YOU GOT VERY CLEAR GOALS AND OBJECTIVES?

This is a key point that we have already considered, but it is worth making again. People need to know what the team is for. A great team knows this and sometimes has a sense of mission, but most people need to have some milestones for their progress. There also need to be some metrics so that teams and the individuals in them can monitor their progress. As we saw in the case study examples, once people own the numbers they will very often surprise you with their willingness to do something about improving them. And in order to do that you need to ensure that they have the resources to do their jobs and be prepared to protect them from management scrutiny long enough to take some risks and make some improvements.

5. WHAT CAN YOU DO ABOUT TEAM SPIRIT?

This is an elusive concept. Many people have experienced team spirit but few of us would like to try to define it. I have steered clear of discussing sports examples, but this is one area where we see their relevance. Great sports teams believe in themselves and their ability to win in a way that can enable them to defeat opponents who, on paper, appear much stronger than themselves. You cannot create team spirit, but you can do a lot to provide the conditions for it to flourish. You can develop a sense of pride by helping people to notice and reflect on their achievements; you can respect everyone in the team equally; you can organize celebrations; you can make up awards and present them. You can define a common enemy if it helps, and allow in-jokes and cliquiness in the team if you want to. The point is that this is an on-going process and you need to seize your opportunities to develop rather than demolish team spirit.

6. DO YOU UNDERSTAND TEAM DYNAMICS?

Team dynamics is not just psycho-babble. It has very useful insights to offer if you are trying to fix an ailing team or set up a functioning one. A group of people are not a team; it is a group that may or may not get beyond the formation stage. Tuckman's forming, storming, norming, and performing framework might sound corny but you need to pay attention to it. If you try to rush people through the phases you are only storing up trouble for later. And if you insist on doing team-building activities with a mature team because something is going wrong don't be surprised if it backfires on you. Mature teams almost certainly don't need to build bridges over rivers or go paintballing. They probably need a bit of space to draw breath and a constructive conversation carried out in the spirit of improvement rather than recrimination. But this is easier said than done. Dealing with people's emotions is tricky, and this is another reason why you shouldn't enter into teamworking unless you really are committed to it. You need to think about entrances and exits to the team, and about how you will handle different levels of seniority in a group of people who are supposed to be working as equals. You need to be sensitive to hidden agendas and able to work through them by treating people as adults. Paying attention to process in groups is vital. You need to concentrate on how people say things as well as what they say, and on those people who are not saying anything. There are lots of tools to help you understand what's going on – from Belbin's team-type inventory to psychometric tools like the Myers–Briggs index. The point is what you do with the information. Whatever you do, you should do it with sensitivity and genuine concern for the welfare of the people in your team.

7. DO YOU PLAY TO STRENGTHS?

Great teams are interdependent. They understand that people like to do certain sorts of work and don't like doing others. Only bullies insist that people do things they don't like doing because it's good for them or for the organization. Most people understand that they have to do some things for the good of the organization that they might not choose to do, but they resent it when their jobs change entirely to suit the company. There was a vivid example of this when banks and building societies insisted on their front-line counter staff becoming salespeople. Friendly, helpful people who liked giving customer service were not necessarily temperamentally suited to trying to on-sell products to regular clients going about their business.

Good team leaders will play to strengths but they will also have an eye to the future and will seek to develop talent. They will celebrate rather than squash diversity. We think of diversity as being about race, gender, age, and so on, and this is vitally important, particularly in the context of the global economy as we have seen. But diversity can also be a bit more low key. Diversity can be about different working styles, and it is worth thinking about how much leeway you can give people on how they do their work, how they organize their work space, and how they manage their time. Uniformity and consistency are great, but sometimes they lead to group think and stagnation. It might be worth loosening up a bit sometimes.

Finally, it might be worth thinking about the people who just want to turn up, do a decent day's work, and go home. These people hardly ever get mentioned in the management literature, but they are present in every organization and can cause major headaches for team leaders under pressure to have a high-performing team of highly motivated individuals. These are the people who in performance management talks don't want to do courses or take on extra responsibility. They are the team leader's nightmare. But the irony is that they are great to have on a team. As Steve Jobs says, great teams ship, and producing results without at least some people who just want to get on and do the job is difficult. So, does the diversity in your team include these people? And can you find them the space to do what they do well and then leave them alone?

8. ARE YOU WILLING TO GET YOUR HANDS DIRTY OCCASIONALLY?

There is a difference of opinion about the role of the team leader. In the past people have often been promoted to supervisory level because they were particularly good at their job rather than because they showed any leadership qualities. And in the past they were advised to rein in any desire to go back to doing the job. Then, for a while in the 1980s, we had the rise of the professional manager who could parachute into any job in any sector with no specialist knowledge except that of how to run the numbers. Both of these approaches led to a certain disenchantment in the staff left to do the work. For years people working in teams have said to me on training courses and in interviews that what they most value in a leader is approachability, but close behind came specialist knowledge or an ability to do the job. This does not mean that team members expect the leader to *do* the job, but they have more respect if they think their leader is able to do it, and their loyalty is generally increased if, when the pressure is on, the leader shows a willingness to roll up their sleeves and help out. This might not always be because the work is piling up. Sometimes team leaders might want to do some of the actual work so that they understand it well enough to lobby on behalf of the team for more resources or some other kind of help. And sometimes they might want to do it to provide cover for a team member or members to do something else, such as some sort of development activity like being on a project team. There might be a temptation for new team leaders to go back to the job when they feel a bit out of their depth or overwhelmed by their new responsibilities, but this is not that common an occurrence, and it is worth taking the risk for the bonuses that a little hands-on activity can bring.

9. DO YOU HAVE CLEARLY IDENTIFIED WORKING NORMS?

It is surprising that little things can undermine team performance. Even those teams who are set to put a dent in the universe can come unstuck over the coffee rota. Make sure that you are very clear about levels of formality – are you a formal or informal team? And make sure that you address the serious issues, too. Do you have a late-night, long-hours culture? What is your line on saying "no" to requests from outside the group? And, of course, ideally you will take these decisions collectively.

10. DO YOU TREAT PEOPLE AS YOU WOULD LIKE TO BE TREATED?

This rule does not just apply to teamworking, it is a rule for most aspects of organizational life. The very best way to lead a team is to ask yourself how you would like to be led. The answer that you are likely to give yourself is that you would like to be treated with respect, given some idea of what kind of job you are doing, given appropriate training, be paid fairly, and then left to get on with it. If that's what you want it's probably what they want. Treating people as human beings is the absolute key to having a high-performance team.

Frequently Asked Questions (FAQs)

Q1: What's the difference between a team and a work-group?

A: A workgroup is made up of individuals working together to pool resources, knowledge, and skills. It will almost certainly have a single leader who makes all the decisions and does all the maintenance jobs like work scheduling and HR duties. These groups often work extremely well. A team, in contrast, is made up of interdependent people who bring a blend of skills and knowledge and could not work without each other. They have a very clear collective vision of where they are going and how they will get there and why they need each other to achieve their goals. They make their own decisions and manage themselves. While they report to a manager they could function on their own for extended periods if they had to. For more information on this see Chapter 2.

Q2: What's the best way to develop an effective team?

A: The very best way to develop a team is to give the members a strong sense of what they are trying to achieve collectively, to ensure that they have adequate resources, to train them, and then get out of their way! See Chapters 6 and 7 for more on this.

Q3: Why isn't my team working well together?

A: Because so many managers have a sentimental attachment to the idea that organizations are rational places where people work under the direct influence of their heads rather than their hearts team building rarely gets done. Your team probably doesn't really know what it is trying to achieve or where it fits into the larger organization. Is it cutting blocks of stone or building cathedrals? Or, equally likely, is there a personality clash which is getting in the way of its performance? You'll have to be brave and sort it out. See Chapter 8 for more ideas about the hidden dynamics in teams.

Q4: What does a good team leader do?

A: The smart answer to this is that the team leader doesn't do anything – the team does; but, more helpfully, a good team leader does what the team needs them to do. An inexperienced team will need a lot of help and support, whereas an established team will need some stretching and motivating. Your input is likely to be technical with a new team or a new job, and supportive as the team becomes established. See Chapters 8 and 10 for more ideas on how to be a great team leader.

Q5: Does every organization need to have teams?

A: No. You need to think long and hard about why you want to set up teams. You should not do it just because your competitors have set up self-managed teams. On the other hand, competitive advantage is increasingly likely to occur in groups of people developing and sharing expert knowledge and the team is the best way to capture that and turn it to your advantage. See Chapter 4 for more information.

Q6: What impact is new technology likely to have on teams?

A: New technology is making teamworking increasingly easy from a logistical point of view. Knowledge management systems and information communications technology are reshaping the nature of our work. Electronic communication means that we can have geographically diverse teams working together in real time or asynchronously. All this is changing the way we configure work and the teams that do it. Chapter 4 explores this further.

Q7: Why do I get the feeling that there's something going on in my team that I can't quite put my finger on?

A: Teams always have a secret life. Team members love or hate each other. People collude to get work done or to sabotage it. You need to be able to diagnose exactly what is getting in the way of team effectiveness. It might also be that yours is a young team where people are jockeying for position or testing the rules. Teams have life cycles like other living things, and this is explored in Chapter 8.

Q8: How are teams likely to work in a global organization?

A: Teams are likely to play a crucial role in globalized firms. Without a global awareness companies run the risk of making costly mistakes which could be avoided if they used diverse teams with diverse members. Technology means that virtual teams will be able to work together easily and effectively. But there's likely to be a downside, too, if organizations try to mix home culture and their own national culture on the ground. These dilemmas are explored in Chapter 5.

Q9: How can I turn a failing team round?

A: First of all you need to audit who you have in the team and measure this against what they are trying to achieve. You could try a tool like Belbin's team types to highlight strengths and weaknesses and get the team to think about how it might improve its work processes. But you might also want to think about what type of team you have got and whether it is making or doing, deciding or managing. Is it clear about the distinctions? If not, is this the cause of the dysfunction? Does your organization have a rugged individualist culture which actively works against cooperation and collaboration, and can you do anything about it? Finally, you might ask if you really need a team at all. This problem is confronted throughout the book.

Q10: What makes a super high-performing team?

A: Super high-performance teams are rare. Unfortunately, they tend to be fleeting groups with a limited lifespan. The teams that made or did things that changed the world were often driven by a passion for an idea or a cause. This is not always possible to reproduce if you are making widgets. But you need to think about how you can introduce an element of this kind of zeal into the team's work. You might have to be creative and rethink the team's work in terms of the contribution it makes to the world, but this kind of vision is often irresistible to teams and might tip them from adequate to outstanding performers. We explore this further in Chapter 6.

Index

Printed and bound by CPI Group (UK) Ltd, Croydon, CR0 4YY

13/04/2025